GATEWAY TO GOD

Simone Weil was born in Paris on February 3rd, 1909. She qualified as a teacher of philosophy in 1931. Between teaching posts she worked in the Renault car factory and in the vineyards. She also spent some time with the Spanish Republican Army on the Catalonian front and experienced the complete invasion of her inner life by the horror of war.

In 1941 she went to live in the south of France, where she worked in the fields while continuing her study of Greek and Hindu philosophy and enlarging her knowledge of Sanskrit. In 1942, after reaching America, she was called to serve the French provisional Government in England. She prepared for them a long study of the reciprocal duties of the individual and the State, later to become famous in English as *The Need for Roots*. She died in 1943, her illness aggravated by her refusal to eat anything more than was given to her compatriots in Occupied France.

Also published in Fount Paperbacks

Simone Weil
WAITING ON GOD

SIMONE WEIL

GATEWAY TO GOD

EDITED BY DAVID RAPER
with the collaboration of
MALCOLM MUGGERIDGE AND
VERNON SPROXTON

Collins
FOUNT PAPERBACKS

First published in Fontana Books 1974
Second Impression September 1975
Third Impression October 1978
Published by Fount Paperbacks 1985

Made and printed in Great Britain by
William Collins Sons & Co Ltd Glasgow

ACKNOWLEDGMENTS

The editor and publisher wish to thank the following:

Mr Leslie Paul for permission to quote his poem 'Lady whose grave I own' from *Journey to Connemara and other Poems* published by Outposts Publications.

Routledge & Kegan Paul Ltd and the University of Massachusetts Press for permission to use extracts from *Oppression and Liberty*; Routledge & Kegan Paul Ltd. and G. P. Putnam's Sons for permission to use extracts from *The Need for Roots* and for permission to reproduce *Letter to a Priest*; Routledge & Kegan Paul Ltd. for permission to use extracts from *Intimations of Christianity among the Ancient Greeks* and *The Notebooks of Simone Weil*.

Oxford University Press for permission to use extracts from *Selected Essays 1934-43*, *On Science, Necessity, and the Love of God*, *Seventy Letters*, and *First and Last Notebooks*.

Editions Gallimard for permission to translate 'The Gate', 'Last Text', 'Theory of the Sacraments' and other extracts from *Pensées sans ordre concernant l'amour de Dieu* © Editions Gallimard 1962, and an extract from *La condition ouvrière* © Editions Gallimard 1951.

The BBC for permission to reproduce the dialogue between André Weil and Malcolm Muggeridge.

CONTENTS

FOREWORD

by Malcolm Muggeridge

In the somewhat sparse literature of our time relating to the Question Why, contrasting with the Question How's enormous yield, Simone Weil's *Waiting on God* is a pearl. I find myself turning to it again and again, and never in vain. Her writings altogether have brought me more comfort and illumination than those of any other contemporary. So, it is welcome news indeed that another selection has been made from her – considering how troubled and afflicted her short life was – astoundingly large output. I was honoured to be asked to contribute a foreword to this new selection, and gratefully seize the opportunity thereby provided of recommending to others what has so enriched my own life. Her insights, far from becoming obsolete, have only grown more relevant with the passing years; the mounting tragedy of Western Man and the ever-accelerating decomposition of his civilization, serve to underline the urgency of what she had to say.

I sometimes think there must be a Celestial Intelligence Service which, like mundane ones, plants stay-behind agents in areas where enemy occupation – in this case, the Devil's – may be expected. Lear, in his final moment of illumination, when at last he sees through the buffooneries of power, the *opera bouffe* of the ego and the melodrama of the will, speaks of how he and Cordelia will now be able to take upon themselves the mystery of things as though they were God's spies. Is there perhaps a hint here of the same notion? In any case, if there are these stay-behind agents planted by a Celestial Intelligence Service, Simone was certainly one of them. She even seems to have had a premonition of something of the kind herself. In her letter to Fr Perrin explaining why, though Christ has taken possession of her, she still cannot feel it is right for her to be baptized and join the

Church, she writes of how, at a time when materialism is taking over the world, God may still want there to be some men and women who have given themselves to him, and yet remain outside the Church. This, to an old Intelligence hand, contains a suggestion of building up cover – a stay-behind agent's first requirement.

As new readers will discover, the light Simone shines makes everything seem, at once, reassuringly recognizable and so luminous as to be heavenly; like looking down on a landscape one knows well when the sun is rising. An idea becomes truly comprehensible, Tolstoy says, only when we are aware of it in our soul; when it gives us the feeling that we knew it already and were simply recalling it. This was how he felt when he read the Gospels – 'It all seemed so familiar; it seemed that I had known it all long ago, that I had only forgotten it.' I felt exactly the same when I first began to read Simone Weil; the great mysteries, like the stupendous drama of the Passion and the necessity of affliction, are seen through a window of time in the perspective of eternity. In this, I might compare her with Mother Teresa, who likewise gives God's universal love a homely and familiar face. They are both pilgrims of the absolute – Simone of absolute truth, and Mother Teresa of absolute love; the two, of course, amounting to the same thing.

For my own first acquaintance with Simone Weil, I am beholden to the late Richard Rees, her dedicated translator and interpreter; he and I being both friends of George Orwell, another pilgrim of the absolute. Rees' *A Sketch for a Portrait* is, I should say, at any rate for English readers, far the best book on her. He had exactly the right temperament for the task he took on of making Simone's ideas comprehensible and palatable to Anglo-Saxons. An ardent francophile himself (he served with the French Merchant Marine in the war of 1939-45), he yet had, in his disposition, and even appearance, a touch of Cervantes' Knight of the Woeful Countenance which enabled him to understand that what might seem at times a certain ultra-seriousness in Simone was by no means the same as ultra-solemnity. After all, Don Quixote, too, was a pilgrim of the absolute. Incidentally, I was interested to learn, in conversation with Simone's brother André, a formidably brilliant mathematician, that when they were young together, she was by no means given to over-seriousness; rather, gay, vivacious and cheerful.

Because she died young and in desolate circumstances, there is a tendency to think of her life as tragic and wasted. On the contrary, it was triumphant. How could it be otherwise for someone who once said that the only human being she ever envied was the bad thief of the trio crucified together on Golgotha; that higher than that she could not aspire? The *soi-disant* liberation of France that she did not live to see would anyway have broken her heart. Instead, she has helped all of us who did see it, and who love and revere her, to reach after another kind of liberation; the only authentic and lasting kind there is – on a Cross.

'This world is the closed door. It is a barrier, and at the same time it is the passage-way.'[1]

(*Notebooks*, p. 492)

THE GATE

by Simone Weil

Open the gate and we shall see the orchards,
We shall drink from cool springs where the moon leaves
  her trace.
The long road is burning hot, unfriendly to strangers.
We wander without knowledge and can find ourselves
  no place.

We want to see flowers. We are so thirsty here.
Waiting and suffering, we are now before the gate.
If we must, we will break it open with our blows.
We press and we push, but we cannot shift its weight.

We must languish, be patient and watch in vain.
We look upon the gate, shut fast, unbreakable.
We fix on it our gaze; tormented, we weep;
Overwhelmed by time's heaviness, we see it still.

The gate is there before us; what use is it to want?
It is better to give up hope and go away.
We shall never enter. We are tired of seeing it.
When the gate opened, so much silence came through

That no orchard or flower appeared to our view;
Just the vast expanse of void and light,
Which filled our hearts as it burst into sight,
And bathed our eyes almost blind in the dust.

(Pensées sans ordre)

LADY WHOSE GRAVE I OWN

by Leslie Paul

(for Simone Weil, died 1943)

Ah Simone, was it love of God that struck you down,
Or the more compelling love of men?
There is an affliction of the body too,
    which trembles in the eyes,
In the palm's sweat, the straight but straying hair,
Unguarded tongue and makes unlovely
That which loves with such a fever
The body's broken by a rigor.
If you had loved less, cared less!
Caring and loving all
Made certain that slow fall.

Simone, I know the Martha tribe that labours
Down the years to win reward,
The washing-up that has polemical intent,
Twice-scrubbed floors: knitting feverish against
The too-late hours; the sullen glance through
    misted spectacles
That hungers for and mulishly rejects the cherished word
Thinking – if you do not see my works are love,
Get out of my way. I'm just a doormat for you.

There can be too much urgency to give of love.
Those workman's boots and graceless jumpers
The endless cigarettes and rough political debates
The redflag marches on the local Mairie,
That mastery of Sophocles and Marx.
Spoke of another hunger than – give my brilliant
    wit the floor:
The panic flight of mind, the long night's fever
That there was only age and barrenness ahead.

It is a sad thing that so much we carry in our hearts
    and hands,
Gifts profligate on our poor shoulders
Are soon like broken things rejected. What point
In birth and growing and eager learning
If there is no human answer to our burning?
But was it for prams and nightie promiscuity
Pomaded Paris husband and the marital tiff
Bourgeois sons in love with their moustaches
You really longed?
Or the Promethean task
The North-West passage of the bruised and hungry soul?

(This is my body: is it given for me?)

It is the mark of the afflicted that
Their own sin's endurable
But they carry into heartbreak
The burden of another's pain,
And more, they are all gravity,
So stricken
Beyond all earthly hope is their despair.

The complacency of the unafflicted
Is more than they can stomach
The adolescent sniggers, the casual lovers
In shadowed arcades, the faceless men in faultless suits
In the Kremlins of power.

And so, Simone, lady whose grave I own,
The migraine, the nausea without cessation,
The Solesmes masses beating on the brain,
The iron will to shrug off so much suffering—
This we know.

          But tell us godly Simone
Of the waiting till the Saviour came again.

Was this the real affliction,
The cross you had to bear,
That you were simply what you were?

INTRODUCTION

by David Raper

It is thirty years since a young Frenchwoman died in a sanatorium in Ashford, Kent. Those years have witnessed the increasing discovery of a legacy of thinking and writing which is quite remarkable in its penetration and power. No less impressive is the size of this legacy, filling at least sixteen volumes of French, and also its range, which extends through the philosophy and religion of both East and West, politics, the natural sciences, mathematics, history, literature, folklore, mythology and even astrology, to the creation of a play and some poems. Simone Weil lived, suffered, and spoke through the ambiguity and emergency of her time, and achieved a conception of absolute good that left her outside every political party and religious institution, every modern school of philosophy, and every *milieu* in which that perfection was compromised or disbelieved. She has been called 'a witness to the absolute'. She could also be called an 'outsider' – an outsider, quite literally, *par excellence*.

Hers is not a name, like that of Albert Camus, which is on a wide range of generally well-informed lips, though, by the way, Camus himself did much to secure the publication of her writings and once said that any real renewal of European life would have to take her insights into account. Nor is it a name like that of Dietrich Bonhoeffer, which is regularly heard in critical Christian quarters and considered a source of a new direction in theology. In fact the occasional coupling of her name with Bonhoeffer's must be regarded with suspicion. Certainly both, in the context of personal involvement in the crisis of the Nazi war, produced notions fundamentally challenging to the prevalent modes of Christian consciousness and religiosity, and died before they themselves could refine and develop them. However, Bonhoeffer's concerns appear to belong very much to a post-Kantian and post-Barthian framework of thought (the use of the word 'religion', for example) whose seeds of secularism lay in the biblical tradition, whereas Simone Weil's concerns belong much more to pre-Enlightenment and non-biblical areas of religion and philosophy, particularly the ancient Greek and, in her latter years, the ancient Far Eastern worlds. Her name on the twentieth-century European scene is very much one to be said on its own. Its connotation should be that which comes, incidentally, with her family's and friends' pronunciation of it, as in the French *veille*, with its association of 'waiting' and 'keeping vigil'.

Such was the theme of *Waiting on God*, an earlier selection of her religious writings to which this one is conceived as a successor. In that volume her personal position, as one of attention particularly outside the organized body of Christians, was somewhat to the fore. In the present selection there is less emphasis on the personal drama of 'waiting', as was supplied, for example, by the letters to Père Perrin, but more on the total intellectual view of the one who waits and on the perception and analysis of the situation in which the waiting is done. Concern is therefore with knowing the nature of God, as the Good; knowing the nature of the world, as Necessity; and having a questioning awareness of the social and institutional structures which may mediate or confuse attention, such as 'religion' and 'church'.

For these three concerns Simone Weil's own poem 'La Porte' provides the right image and keynote, that of the gate or doorway. God is the absolute good, and the world is the gateway to it, so are religion, philosophy, art and science. What is imperative for the traveller at the gate is that he should maintain his sense of the absoluteness of what lies beyond, and also the integrity and honesty with which his account of it is applied to life in the world. In these writings we see someone with magnificence and with pathos following that imperative.

The *pensées* or selected thoughts, which follow Vernon Sproxton's biographical essay, are an attempt to put in a relatively consecutive form the principal elements of Simone Weil's intellectual account of reality and the human condition. They vary in length and form from whole short articles, or sections of articles, to single sayings in note form. The juxtaposition and editing of these thoughts, which with some writers would be unjust and presumptuous, is legitimate and perhaps even necessary in the case of Simone Weil. What amounts to a single world view, with both its paradoxes and its logic, does appear through her writings, even though she died before setting it out formally herself. However, there is evidence that she did envisage a collection of thoughts, for which she actually wrote a short narrative prologue (which appears in both published translations of her notebooks). In this selection I have tried to make explicit the sequence which is implicit in her writings.

The predominance of *First and Last Notebooks* (abbreviated to *FLN*), published in 1970, as a source for the *pensées* can be explained in two ways. First, it includes the last collections of Simone Weil's notebook material to be translated into English, the notes written in New York and London in the last months of her life. These, therefore, may be less well known than those in the two volumes of *Notebooks* published earlier, and in the selection from them entitled *Gravity and Grace*. Secondly *First and Last Notebooks* contain much of what was most remarkable and stimulating in her religious thought.

The notebooks were really her workshop, in which she tested, forged, or simply recorded, ideas, and in which she wrote down questions, connections, speculations and reactions to reading. They owe their existence probably to a precept of Alain, one of her philosophy teachers, who urged his pupils to keep a day-to-day record of not only their thoughts but also the contrary propositions by which they were tested. Because of this last factor one has to beware of using a single note out of context as an indication of her mind, and there is certainly no substitute for reading the notebooks as a whole. However, when one does read them in entirety, a coherent picture does emerge, complementary to that which is found in her more formal writings. The present selection endeavours to convey the picture given in both.

Various editorial idiosyncrasies, such as the reversal of the order of some notes which were quite near each other in the original, can be explained by the desire to present a logically, but not chronologically, developing theme. The passages on Work (translated by Patricia Miles) are of particular value in showing Simone Weil's view of physical labour, which she held to be the spiritual centre of rightly organized corporate life. The 'Theory of the Sacraments' and 'Last Text' (to which, along with the other extracts from *Pensées sans ordre concernant l'amour de Dieu*, I have supplied a translation) are included as examples of her religious thinking specifically in a Christian context. The 'Theory of the Sacraments', which was sent from London to Maurice Schumann in 1943, is an interesting application of her accounts of the absolute good and the human condition to a particular element of religion. The so-called 'Last Text', whose history is somewhat mysterious but which must date from the end of her life, shows her state of feeling, and also what she saw as her intellectual role, with regard to institutional and confessional Christianity.

The essays on the love of God require little introduction. They were all three probably written in Marseilles between October 1940 and May 1942. The third one, 'Additional pages on the Love of God and Affliction', is in fact the second part of an essay on that topic, but was discovered after the first part had been published. It reads well on its own, but the first part can be found in *Waiting on God*. The translation of these three pieces from *On Science, Necessity and the Love of God* (also of the passages in the previous section from *Selected Essays, Seventy Letters*, and *First and Last Notebooks*) is by the late Sir Richard Rees, whose contribution, as translator, editor and interpreter, to the understanding of Simone Weil in the English-speaking world is of the highest order.

The *Letter to a Priest* dates from Simone Weil's time in New York. The priest in question was Père Couturier who, most interestingly, was later to do pioneering ecumenical work within the Roman Catholic Church which earned him the description 'the apostle of unity'. Couturier had no chance to comment on the letter, since his correspondent left for England the day after he received it. It is placed as the last item in this volume, so that it should be read with the view expressed in the earlier items already in mind. This is because the *Letter* does have a strong negative note. However, its value and ultimate intent are positive. The level of feeling in it indicates the degree to which Simone Weil did want the sacraments, and did want to stand within a social and cultural growing of roots which spread from the inspiration of Christ throughout the whole universe of experience. The manner and extent of Christ-centredness in her thought, evident in the other writings, must not be forgotten when one reads the *Letter*. However, the elaboration of points of conflict between her mind and the apparatus of institutional Christianity cannot be ignored, and surely represents the obstacles that face any future development of real ecumenical understanding both within the Christian tradition, and between the Christian and other religious traditions.

PILGRIM OF THE ABSOLUTE

An Outline of Simone Weil's Life

by Vernon Sproxton

'Just as the top layer in a case of herrings is crushed and spoilt, and the fruit next to the crate is bruised and worthless, so too in every generation there are certain men who are on the outside and are made to suffer from the packing case, who only protect those who are in the middle . . . There is a bird called the stormy-petrel, and that is what I am; when in a generation storms begin to gather, individuals of my type appear.'

That was what Søren Kierkegaard wrote about himself in 1845. But precisely the same images could be used to describe Simone Weil. She was, in every sense of the word, *an outsider*. And she was a stormy-petrel, too, heralding the approach of troubled times. She had an almost seismographic sensitivity to rumblings in the world about her. It was Simone de Beauvoir who said of her, 'Her heart would miss a beat for something that happened at the other end of the earth.' And it was such happenings which always hurt and ultimately destroyed her.

She was French. And to say that is to say much more than that she was born in France – in Paris, in 1909; for her brief life reflected and encompassed genius which was uniquely French. Some of the notes in her *Cahiers* possess the lapidary and seminal quality of Pascal's *Pensées*. Her ruthless honesty of thought is reminiscent of the *Method* of Descartes. The almost romantic awe in which she held manual labour springs directly from Rousseau. A man watching her leading a march of unemployed miners said that for the first time in his life he understood Joan of Arc. She was attracted as if by a magnet to the poor and down-trodden, a latter-day Saint Vincent or Curé d'Ars. Montaigne lives again in her passion to know the truth and Paul Valéry in her search for *le moi pur*. For, energizing all her work, there was an intense desire for inner purification. Gabriel Marcel called her 'a pilgrim of the absolute.'

She was Jewish, and she resented the fact. She had never been exposed to any Jewish rites or practices. Her parents were both agnostics. In fact she did not even know that she was Jewish until she was quite old. But the shock was enough to blind her to some of the most profound truths of the Old Testament. It may even have induced in her a rejection of 'the body', and a distaste for physical contact which makes her sound at times like a Manichean. But when people called her 'the red virgin of the tribe of Levi' they were tracing her spiritual lineage back to Amos and Hosea. All other things Jewish she might and did disclaim, but she retained the gift of prophecy.

She was bourgeois and urban. Her parents came from Alsace and were fluent in German. Her father was a genial doctor in general practice. Her mother was a determined and possessive woman of acute intelligence. A skilled manager and negotiator, she would let nothing stand in the way of what she thought was necessary for the intellectual and physical development of her children. She planned and protected Simone's life in a manner which, even thirty years ago, must have been unwarranted and excessive. (Those who have a taste for finding the seeds of genius in early childhood might find this relationship a happy hunting-ground.) But if the home was something of an intellectual forcing-house, it was also happy, full of fun, and sometimes even gay. Almost every year the family would leave their comfortable home near the fashionable Luxembourg Gardens and take a holiday in the country or by the sea. A child of Simone's intelligence would be quick to perceive that others did not live as they lived. And though some of the stories of her early asceticism are clearly legendary, from an early age she developed a sympathy with the poor which was never to leave her.

She was *une malade*. She had several bouts of sickness as a child but in her teens she developed a chronic complaint which never left her: crippling headaches, the cause of which was never diagnosed. There were various explanations:

sinusitis and allied conditions. Today psychosomatic factors might have been cited: tensions springing from the relationship with her mother, or her attitude to her own body. She once said that God had cut her out badly. And she went to great lengths to prove that she could do anything anybody else could do, even to the extent of playing rugger! But speculation is idle. Books may one day be written about Simone's headaches as in the past they have been written about Darwin's stomach troubles. The fact is that they were always with her and sometimes made her life a veritable hell.

She was clever. Spurred on, for a time, by an envy of her elder brother, and by a determination not to be excluded from the kingdom of truth, she quickly developed an analytic brilliance which swept her through the portals of France's most distinguished academic institutions: first, the Lycée Henri IV, where the redoubtable Alain became her *maître de pensée*, and whose influence was vital, though she differed from him on many points; and later the Ecole Normale Supérieture, where she was one of the first women to be admitted and she came under the influence of nobody but herself. Contemporaries remember her well: a shock of ill-kempt hair and unbecoming spectacles, carelessly rather than shabbily dressed; intense, ceaselessly arguing, citing facts and figures, laughing, from time to time breaking out into malicious wit; rallying students to support out-of-work miners, collecting funds to help striking railwaymen; assailing people in the quadrangle with 'Have you heard what "they" are doing to the workers in St Etienne . . . or Shanghai . . . or Rabat?'

She threw herself in with the Left and became absorbed in workers' education. She was profoundly influenced by Marx but, in spite of the fact that she once smuggled out of Berlin into Paris a list of all the known German Trotskyites, she never joined the Party. She dreaded the collective, partly because she was a congenital loner, partly because in the perspective of history she loathed nothing more than what she called the Great Beast, exemplified by Imperial Rome and Exclusive Israel, but also because she had a deep feeling for the priority of the personal. She did not, however, join up with the Personalist Movement – led by her contemporary

Emmanuel Mounier – an inspired attempt to shore up the tottering Third Republic, because it was tied up with Catholicism, and Them.

At the Ecole she made an impressive intellectual mark, and a life of academic brilliance seemed assured when she graduated in 1931 – a year of ill omen for Europe in many respects. She had hoped to get a post in some industrial area like Le Havre. Instead she was sent to Le Puy, an enchanting tourist town in the middle of France, to teach philosophy at the girls' lycée. She was soon in trouble. Those were the days when a minister of education prided himself that he knew at any moment of any day precisely what a child of any age was learning. Simone had her own ideas about curricula, and even inferred that the set texts were erroneous.

The girls found her manner and her dress odd. She sat rigidly in the desk looking straight ahead of her and spoke in a monotonous voice. She used a method which was unfamiliar, making her pupils write short notes on many subjects which she assiduously corrected and discussed with them, making them clarify and distinguish again and again until they were virtually exhausted. Soon she had the girls on her side. They were calling her 'our Simone'. Her methods were effective. But they were irregular. And worse was to follow.

Immediately she had settled in Le Puy she made contact with trades union groups in the mining region of St Etienne not many miles away. Each Thursday, when the school was closed, she would go over and spend the day consulting with leaders, collating information on conditions and pay, suggesting courses of action, advising on the presentation of cases, and teaching the unemployed. In the evening she would meet with the leaders of teachers' associations in the café Victor Hugo and, long after it had closed, she would go on working into the night, snatching a few hours' sleep on one of the benches before taking the first train back to Le Puy. She quickly became the miners' darling. No event, whether it were a march or a social evening was complete without her. Four ex-thugs acted as a self-appointed bodyguard and, when she was speaking, prevented the police from moving her on. She was never happier than when she was waving the

Red Flag at the front of a procession.

One day there was a demonstration of strikers at Le Puy in the square in front of the school. When she had finished teaching she went to join them. The bourgeois burghers were incensed. There was a public scandal, and the papers came down against her. The parents of her own class, urged on by their desolate daughters, made a spirited attempt to save her. But it was no use. At the end of the summer term she had to go.

If you go to those parts now you will find aged, hard-boiled, dyed-in-the-wool trades unionists who weep at the mention of her name. And middle-aged ladies take from their bottom drawers dog-eared old essays and point to her writing and the holes burnt in the paper from her ceaseless smoking. They knew that they had been in touch with a being of exceptional quality. 'When Simone left us,' one of them said, 'something died.'

She got another post; this time at Auxerre, near enough to St Etienne to keep in touch with her comrades, and convenient for Paris which she visited from time to time. More frequently, however, people visited her, and the unpretentious café over which she had rooms occasionally was the scene of animated arguments between prominent people of the Left. She was able to devote more time to writing, and some of her more important articles date from this time. She wrote with a sense of desperate urgency, eating next to nothing, and living mainly on wine, coffee, and cigarettes. Whenever there was a strike at a local factory the workers would seek her out to ask her advice. Immediately she got home from school she was among them, often in bare feet. A good proportion of her salary went to helping needy cases, and she got rid of most of the furniture her mother had provided. The results of her teaching were catastrophic: most of her pupils failed their *baccalauréat*, and the course was brought to an end.

She was to teach again, from time to time – at Roanne, Bourges, and St-Quentin – but from now on it became clear that between Simone and established, formal education there lay an unbridgeable gulf. The sense of solidarity with the workers of the world (which holidays in Germany and Spain had confirmed) made her wish to sample industrial life at first hand. She asked for a year off, no doubt to the relief of the pedagogues, and she took a job in a factory, rented a simple room, and tried to live on her wages. The factory made electric motors and her first task was to press out small metal pieces. She was so maladroit – she could scarcely roll a cigarette – that she had great difficulty in keeping up a profitable pace. The nagging insistence to get the rate doubled, and the conditions in which she worked exhausted her body and numbed her spirit. She knew, of course, that she could pull out and go back home. But she stuck it out. The experience branded her for ever as a slave, and she caught something of the desolation of people for whom 'the only hope for tomorrow is being allowed to spend another day like today.' It is therefore not surprising that during the rash of industrial strife which paralysed France during 1936 an active part in organizing the metal-workers' strike was played by Simone Alphonse Weil. At the same time, under the pen-name S. Galois, she was writing about her experiences in *Révolution Prolétarienne*!

In June of the same year she was back in Spain, in the uniform of the Anarchist CNT Brigade, in spite of her pacifism, fighting on the side of the Reds. Whether she actually fired a rifle is uncertain; she was congenitally so clumsy that her own side were probably just as vulnerable as the Royalists! And it was an accident with boiling cooking oil which gave her parents an excuse for retrieving their wounded daughter some three months later. So she did not stay long, but long enough to experience to the full the physical hardship, horror, and political corruption of civil war. She saw that clean principles and fine theories when clothed with real flesh and blood take on a different aspect. 'I no longer felt compelled to take part in a war which was not, as it had appeared at the outset, a war of starving peasants against rich landlords and their priestly accomplices; but a war between Russia, Germany, and Italy.'

Several left-wing intellectuals found themselves caught up in the same moral confusion, notably Arthur Koestler, who laid it bare in *Darkness at Noon*, *Arrival and Departure*, and *Spanish Testament*. One of his characters, caught in the dilemma of the cruel activism of the Commissar on the one hand and the useless quietism of the Yogi on the other says, 'Perhaps a new God is going to be born.' Somewhere about this time Simone Weil turned more and more towards religion.

Hitherto, Simone had assumed that her ethical attitude to life had been a Christian one, but she had no specific religious experiences. When the question of God was raised by her students she tended to ignore it on the grounds of insufficient data. Though certain Christian characters appealed to her – she fell in love with St Francis as soon as she heard of him – she had no experience of the transcendent; and she had not even read about the mystics. Nevertheless, from time to time, she found herself open to what nowadays would be called 'disclosure situations'. She was deeply impressed by simple Portuguese fisherfolk processing round their boats by candle-light whilst they sang religious songs. She realized that Christianity is first and foremost a religion of slaves. Whilst visiting St Francis' chapel in Assisi she was overcome by a sense of awe which threw her to her knees for the first time in her life. In Bourges cathedral she once found herself strangely moved by Gregorian chanting. But these could be construed as what Kierkegaard would have called pre-religious experiences, a mixture of aesthetics and ethics.

It was the aesthetic element of Gregorian chanting which drew her to Solesmes to spend Holy Week and Easter in 1938. She had suffered a general breakdown in health, and wished to experience the Passiontide offices and the incomparable chanting of the monks of the Benedictine abbey. During one of them she was so overcome by a crippling headache that each sound hit her spirit like a blow. But by an extreme effort of attention she 'was able to rise above this wretched flesh, to leave it to suffer by itself, heaped up in a corner, and to find a pure and perfect joy in the unimaginable beauty of the chanting and the words'. During the course of those services the thought of the Passion of Christ – about which in future she could not think without committing the sin of envy – entered her being for once and for all. She met there a young American who introduced her to the work of George Herbert, whose 'Love bade me welcome' impressed her deeply. It became a kind of prayer. She learnt it by heart. At the culmination of a bad headache she would recite it, concentrating on it every atom of her attention. During one such recitation 'Christ came down and took possession of me.' The possibility of such a divine-human encounter had never occurred to her, and she thought it providential that she had not read the mystics, so that the experience could not be part of her fertile imagination.

Simone had now passed through the gateway to God, her own equivalent of Augustine's garden in Milan, and Pascal's night of fire. Some of the luminous truths which were revealed to her lively and original mind during her short Christian pilgrimage are contained in this book. The accidents of history accelerated her progress. When Paris fell in 1940 she left with her parents for Vichy and, later, Marseilles. Not for one moment did she abandon the secular, political world. She even wrote articles for clandestine newspapers. But at the same time she sought guidance from Fr Perrin, a monk at the Dominican convent, whose special office was to help people who might have 'difficulties' with the Pétain régime. In a tiny consultation room, surrounded by second-hand clothing to be doled out to ex-prisoners and fallen women, the two of them talked, 'fellow seekers of the truth'. She developed her theme of 'waiting', waiting on God, of being disposable. She confessed that she loved much of what the Church taught, she adored the Gospel and the Sacraments. She even loved the Church as a guardian of the truth, but as an institution she abhorred it. She had no patience with an organization which guaranteed salvation by a spiritual mechanism and pronounced anathemas on all who did not conform. She preferred to identify herself with those who were outside. She would remain for ever on the threshold, a bell summoning people to church but never entering. She would never be baptized.

It is clear from her *Cahiers* that Marseilles represented a period of furious intellectual energy. Her classical education, her knowledge of Eastern writings, and her awareness of political and social problems were all brought into a fruitful relationship with the enthusiasm of a neophyte's faith. The result was a collection of writings of almost unbelievable maturity and brilliance. Central to everything was the cross.

The resurrection was difficult for her. It would have been easier if it had not happened. 'The cross is sufficient for me.'

Simone was nonetheless restless. She wanted to get to America and thence to England to join the Free French Forces. But there were difficulties, and when she was dismissed from the university, where she held a minor teaching post, under the decree forbidding Jews to hold such positions, she asked Fr Perrin whether he could arrange for her to go into the country as an ordinary labourer. She wanted at first hand to endure the hardships of agricultural workers. Perrin sent her to a Catholic novelist and author, Gustave Thibon, who farmed some land in the vine-growing region of the Ardèche. As a Pétainist Thibon did not relish the prospect of harbouring a Jewess of pronounced left-wing views. The early encounters gave him no ground for comfort. Simone toiled in the vineyards all day, but when she returned home at night she would talk incessantly, always stating her mind with precision, even to the point of social embarrassment. Soon, however, the awkwardness of the relationship wore off, and there developed what Thibon later described as the most illuminating and rewarding friendship of his life. After the family had had supper they would read together the Greek classics, Simone flooding them with a light Thibon had never dreamed of. They learned the Lord's prayer in Greek. Simone used to say it each morning with complete attention. If her mind wandered, even for a second, she would go back to the beginning again. Sometimes as she repeated it she had a sensation of the real presence of Christ.

Soon, however, the Thibons' house became too comfortable, and their company too congenial. She moved into a ramshackle and virtually derelict cottage about a mile away. Here she lived with great frugality, sometimes eating only wild fruit and windfalls. From her pitiful wages she sent donations to political prisoners. Work in the vineyards was for her a kind of hell, and her writing of manual labour as a kind of death is amongst the profoundest and most beautiful of her notes. After a few weeks she moved to another district where, unknown, she could really identify herself with the life of the peasant. Frequently racked with pain, and palpably undernourished, she refused to work shorter hours than the sturdy labourers who were her companions.

Permission came through for the family to leave for America. Thibon went to see her in Marseilles before they sailed. He was shocked by Simone's appearance. She was prematurely bent and old-looking, only her eyes triumphing 'through this shipwreck of beauty'. But her soul, as he described it, was ready to be absorbed into pure being. He had the impression that she was feeding him with light.

In New York she immediately began agitating for a passage to England and, through the good offices of Maurice Schumann, a friend from school-days, and whom she literally badgered into finding a post for her, she found herself in London, working directly under André Philip. Her condition was pitiable, so much so that her landlady in Holland Park thought she must be impoverished and gave her the cheapest rooms she had. She ate next to nothing, and even gave her meagre rations to the children of the house.

She liked London, admired the stoical spirit of the people, and enjoyed many of its institutions, particularly the pubs. Each day she would go to Hill Street, the HQ of the Free French Forces. Part of her duties consisted in monitoring political reports, particularly those that came from Resistance groups. But she had other aims. One was to set up an élite nursing-service which would be available to give succour to the troops immediately they were injured. It was clear that many of them died because help was not swiftly available, and it was a good idea, but for a different sort of war. De Gaulle pronounced it 'mad'. Nothing came of it. The other ambition was to be parachuted into France on some dangerous secret mission. This was equally foolish. She had neither the constitution nor the temperament for such an assignment. The fact that in spite of all her effort and hopes there was to be no tangible way of expressing her desperate sense of brotherhood with the French people reduced her at times to complete despair.

Another job was found for her. She was given the task of drawing up a kind of spiritual testament which could be used as the basis for a constitution for the Fourth Republic. (This was published as *The Need for Roots*.) By any standards it is an astonishing document. All the resources of Simone

Weil's prodigious knowledge and acute intelligence were focused on the problems which post-war politicians would have to face and for the most part have ducked. She saw that the cry for 'rights' echoes as a command to 'duties'. Above all she realized that replacing the idea of truth and justice with that of productivity and utility was an invitation to disaster.

It is doubtful whether anybody, apart from Schumann, took much interest in what she was doing. It was now the winter of 1942-3. Rommel was in full retreat. The battle of North Africa was over. The real agony of Europe was about to begin. Invasion was just around the corner. The tough desperadoes who formed a substantial part of the Free French Forces would not want elegant discussions on the spiritual issues of the peace. Simone must have felt lonely among such company, and her consummate ability at seeing the other side of everybody else's case must have made her a sort of universal enemy. In despair she resigned.

But her letters home remained cheerful. As winter changed into spring and then the peerless summer of 1943 she exulted in the flowers, the people in the parks, and the concerts at the National Gallery. What her parents did not know was that she was writing from hospital. In the middle of April a friend had found her slumped over her desk. She was taken to the Out Patients Department at the Middlesex Hospital and admitted. She had tuberculosis, badly in one lung, and spreading fast. She was also undernourished. The physicians had no doubt that she could be cured. It was a matter of time and the right kind of food to which her condition made her entitled. But they had reckoned without Simone's implacable will. She refused to have a calory more than the paltry rations the French people were being allowed by the Germans. Indeed, she would scarcely eat as much as that, and the hospital records reveal, with scarcely concealed impatience, that she was both a trial and a problem for the doctors.

However, she was able to write and from time to time she received friends. She seems to have been particularly popular with young people. But there is no doubt that she had arrived at the end term of the logic of her life. Weak and emaciated, she asked to be taken to the country – as near to France as possible. A place was found for her at the Grosvenor Sanatorium near Ashford in Kent. When she arrived there she was too ill to be properly examined. She utterly refused to co-operate with any form of treatment. She ate hardly anything. Occasionally she would allow one of the nurses to wet her lips with sherry. When she spoke it was through clenched teeth, presumably to prevent people forcing food into her mouth. It seems as though she felt that in a mysterious way God would use her death. 'Even though the bread of the Host be mouldy, once it is consecrated it is God.' After a week she fell into a deep coma. In the evening of 24 August, her body broken and literally worn out, she died. She was thirty-four.

At the inquest the coroner decided that she had taken her own life by refusing to take food whilst the balance of her mind was disturbed. Not far away from the coroner's court workmen were preparing a pauper's grave. Only a handful of people came down from London for the funeral. There was no priest. A few prayers were said by one of the mourners. Mrs Francis, her landlady, threw on to the coffin a bunch of flowers tied with red, white, and blue ribbon. Then the grave was filled in and grassed over, and for years remained unmarked except by its plot number. Simone had become what she wanted to become: an anonymity, nothing. One is reminded again of Kierkegaard: 'God created everything out of nothing, and everything he wishes to use he first reduces to nothing.' And of that other saint's obscure death which has caught the imagination of our time, Dietrich Bonhoeffer; 'When man is nothing God is mighty.'

Some years after the war a number of distinguished men, mostly writers, subscribed for a simple stone which says simply: Simone Weil, 1909-1943. More recently an unknown donor has attached a small plaque written in Italian: *La mia solitudine l'atrui dolore germivo fino all morte. C.M.* (My solitude held in its grasp the grief of others till my death). Whoever the donor is, and whatever his source may be, he has perfectly understood the life and thought of Simone Weil.

SELECTED 'PENSEES' OF SIMONE WEIL

a. The human situation – between necessity and good

The essential contradiction in the human condition is that man is subject to force, and craves for justice. He is subject to necessity, and craves for the good. It is not his body alone that is thus subject, but all his thoughts as well; and yet man's very being consists in straining towards the good. That is why we all believe that there is a unity between necessity and the good. Some believe that the thoughts of man concerning the good possess the highest degree of force here below; these are known as idealists. They are doubly mistaken, first in that these thoughts are without force, and secondly in that they do not lay hold of the good. These thoughts are influenced by force; so that this attitude is in the end a less energetic replica of the contrary attitude. Others believe that force is of itself directed towards the good; these are idolaters. This is the belief of all material-ists who do not sink into the state of indifference. They are also doubly mistaken; first force is a stranger to and indifferent to the good, and secondly it is not always and everywhere the stronger. They alone can escape these errors who have recourse to the incomprehensible notion that there is a unity between necessity and the good, in other words, between reality and the good, outside this world. These last also believe that something of this unity communicates itself to those who direct towards it their attention and their desire – a notion still more incomprehensible, but verified experimentally. . . .

The facts prove that nearly always men's thoughts are fashioned – as Marx thought – by the lies involved in social morality. Nearly always, but not quite always. That too is certain. Twenty-five centuries ago, certain Greek philosophers, whose very names are unknown to us, affirmed that slavery is absolutely contrary both to reason and to nature. Obvious as are the fluctuations of morality in accordance with time and place, it is equally obvious also that the morality which proceeds directly from mystic thought is one, identical, unchangeable. This can be verified by turning to Egypt, Greece, India, China, Buddhism, the Moslem tradition, Christianity and the folklore of all countries. This morality is unchangeable because it is a reflection of the absolute good that is situated outside this world. It is true that all religions, without exception, have concocted impure mixtures of this morality and social morality, in varying doses. It constitutes nevertheless the experimental proof on earth that the pure transcendental good is real; in other words, the experimental proof of the existence of God.

(*Oppression and Liberty*, pp. 159-61)

There is a reality outside the world, that is to say, outside space and time, outside man's mental universe, outside any sphere whatsoever that is accessible to human faculties.

Corresponding to this reality, at the centre of the human heart, is the longing for an absolute good, a longing which is always there and is never appeased by any object in this world.

Another terrestrial manifestation of this reality lies in the absurd and insoluble contradictions which are always the terminus of human thought when it moves exclusively in this world.

Just as the reality of this world is the sole foundation of facts, so that other reality is the sole foundation of good.

That reality is the unique source of all the good that can exist in this world: that is to say, all beauty, all truth, all justice, all legitimacy, all order, and all human behaviour that is mindful of obligations.

Those minds whose attention and love are turned towards that reality are the sole intermediary through which good can descend from there and come among men.

Although it is beyond the reach of any human faculties, man has the power of turning his attention and love towards it.

Nothing can ever justify the assumption that any man, whoever he may be, has been deprived of this power.

It is a power which is only real in this world in so far as it is exercised. The sole condition for exercising it is consent.

This act of consent may be expressed, or it may not be, even tacitly; it may not be clearly conscious, although it has really taken place in the soul. Very often it is verbally expressed although it has not in fact taken place. But whether expressed or not, the one condition suffices: that it shall in fact have taken place.

To anyone who does actually consent to directing his attention and love beyond the world, towards the reality that exists outside the reach of all human faculties, it is given to succeed in doing so. In that case, sooner or later, there descends upon him a part of the good, which shines through him upon all that surrounds him.

The combination of these two facts – the longing in the depth of the heart for absolute good, and the power, though only latent, of directing attention and love to a reality beyond the world and of receiving good from it – constitutes a link which attaches every man without exception to that other reality.

Whoever recognizes that reality recognizes also that link. Because of it, he holds every human being without any exception as something sacred to which he is bound to show respect.

This is the only possible motive for universal respect towards all human beings. Whatever formulation of belief or disbelief a man may choose to make, if his heart inclines him to feel this respect, then he in fact also recognizes a reality other than this world's reality. Whoever in fact does not feel this respect is alien to that other reality also.

The reality of the world we live in is composed of variety. Unequal objects unequally solicit our attention. Certain people personally attract our attention, either through the hazard of circumstances or some chance affinity. For the lack of such circumstance or affinity other people remain unidentified. They escape our attention or, at the most, it only sees them as items of a collectivity.

If our attention is entirely confined to this world it is entirely subject to the effect of these inequalities, which it is all the less able to resist because it is unaware of it.

It is impossible to feel equal respect for things that are in fact unequal unless the respect is given to something that is identical in all of them. Men are unequal in all their relations with the things of this world, without exception. The only thing that is identical in all men is the presence of a link with the reality outside the world.

All human beings are absolutely identical in so far as they can be thought of as consisting of a centre, which is an unquenchable desire for good, surrounded by an accretion of psychical and bodily matter.

Only by really directing the attention beyond the world can there be real contact with this central and essential fact of human nature. Only an attention thus directed possesses the faculty, always identical in all cases, of irradiating with light any human being whatsoever.

If anyone possesses this faculty, then his attention is in reality directed beyond the world, whether he is aware of it or not.

The link which attaches the human being to the reality outside the world is, like the reality itself, beyond the reach of human faculties. The respect that it inspires as soon as it is recognized cannot be expressed to it.

This respect cannot, in this world, find any form of direct expression. But unless it is expressed it has no existence. There is a possibility of indirect expression for it.

The respect inspired by the link between man and the reality outside the world can be expressed to that part of man which exists in the reality of this world.

The reality of this world is necessity. The part of man which is in this world is the part which is in bondage to necessity and subject to the misery of need.

The one possibility of indirect expression of respect for the human being is offered by men's needs, the needs of the soul and of the body, in this world.

(From 'Draft for a Statement of Human Obligations' in *Selected Essays*, pp. 219-21 translated from *Ecrits de Londres*, Gallimard.)

b. *The absolute good – God*

The essential thing to know about God is that God is the Good. All the rest is secondary. (*Pensées sans ordre*, p. 47)

God is the sole good. All the goods contained in things have their equivalent in God. God is the sole measure of value. (*First and Last Notebooks*, p. 349, translated from *La Connaissance surnaturelle*, Gallimard)

The God is outside this world. (FLN, p. 139)

Only God is the good, therefore only he is a worthy object of care, solicitude, anxiety, longing, and efforts of thought. Only he is a worthy object of all those movements of the soul which are related to some value. Only he has an affinity with that movement towards the good, that longing for the good which is the very centre of my being. (FLN, p. 124)

To know that God is the good or more simply, that the absolute good is the good, and to have faith that the desire for good is self-multiplying in the soul, provided that the soul does not withhold its consent from the operation – these two simple things are enough. Nothing else is needed. (FLN, p. 309)

Outside me there is a good which is superior to me and which influences me for good every time that I desire the good.
Since there is no possible limit to this operation, this external good is infinite; it is God.
And even here it is not a question of belief but of certainty. The thought of the good inevitably involves all these thoughts, and it is impossible not to think of the good.
Since there is no limit to this operation, the soul must finally cease to be, through total assimilation to God. (FLN, p. 310)

God is powerless, except for the equitable and merciful distribution of the good. He can do nothing else. But that is enough.
He has the monopoly of good. He is present himself in everything that effects pure good. Everything which effects

good of a lower order proceeds from the things in which he is present. All authentic good, of whatever order, derives supernaturally from him. Everything which is not directly or indirectly the effect of God's supernatural working is bad or indifferent. (FLN, pp. 122, 123)

Except through the secret and supernatural presence of God (one form of which is the order and beauty of the world . . .) this world can only do what is bad or indifferent.

It can do all possible harm to whatever is not supernaturally protected by the good that issues from God.

The amount of harm it can do where God is present is indicated with perfect veracity in the four Gospels.

To be a Christian has no other meaning than to believe this. (FLN, p. 123)

All goods in this world, all beauties, all truths, are diverse and partial aspects of one unique good. Therefore they are goods which need to be ranged in order. Puzzle games are an image of this operation. Taken all together, viewed from the right point and rightly related, they make an architecture. Through this architecture the unique good, which cannot be grasped, becomes apprehensible.

All architecture is a symbol of this, an image of this.

The entire universe is nothing but a great metaphor. (FLN, p. 98)

c. The reality of absolute good. The 'proof by perfection'

In everything that concerns absolute good and contact with it, the proof by perfection (sometimes wrongly called onto-logical) is not only a valid proof, but it is the only valid one. It follows directly from the very notion of good. It is for good what geometrical demonstration is for necessity. (*Pensées sans ordre*, p. 136)

An experimental ontological proof. I have not the principle of rising in me. I cannot climb to heaven through the air. It is only by directing my thoughts toward something better than myself that I am drawn upwards by this something. If I am really drawn up, this something which draws me is real. No imaginary perfection can draw me upwards even by the fraction of an inch. For an imaginary perfection is mathematically at the same level as I am who imagine it – neither higher nor lower. What draws one up is directing one's thoughts toward a veritable perfection. (*Notebooks*, Vol. II, p. 434)

Essential point of Christianity – (and of Platonism) – :
It is only the thought of perfection that produces any good – and this good is imperfect. If one aims at imperfect good, one does evil.
One cannot really aim at perfection unless it is really possible; so this is the proof that the possibility of perfection exists in this world. (FLN, p. 342)

That God is the good is a certainty. It is a definition. And it is even certain that God – in some way that I do not know – is reality. This is certain, and not a matter of faith. But it is an object of faith that every thought of mine which is a desire for good brings me nearer to the good. It is only by experience that I can test this. And even after the experience it is still not an object of proof but only of faith.
To possess the good consists in desiring the good; therefore the relevant article of faith – which is the sole article of true faith – is concerned with fecundity, with the self-multiplying faculty of every desire for good.
From the mere fact that a part of the soul truly and purely and exclusively desires the good, it follows that at a later point in time a larger part of it will desire the good – unless it refuses to consent to this development.
To believe that is to possess faith. (FLN, p. 307)

But – it will be asked – does this good exist? What does it matter? the things of this world exist, but they are not the good. Whether the good exists or not, there is no other good than the good.
And what is this good? I have no idea – but what does it matter? It is that whose name alone, if I attach my thought to it, gives me the certainty that the things of this world are not goods. If I know nothing more than that name I have no need to know any more, provided only that I know how to use it in this way.
But is it not ridiculous to abandon what exists for some-

thing which perhaps does not exist? By no means, if what exists is not good and if what perhaps does not exist is the good.

But why say 'what perhaps does not exist'? The good certainly does not possess a reality to which the attribute 'good' is added. It has no being other than this attribute. Its only being consists in being the good. But it possesses in fullness the reality of that being. It makes no sense to say the good exists or the good does not exist; one can only say: the good.

The things of this world exist. Therefore I do not detach from them those of my faculties that are related to existence. But since the things of this world contain no good, I simply detach from them the faculty which is related to the good, that is to say, the faculty of love. (FLN, p. 315, 316)

The notion of Good is above the notion of Being and God is Good before even being that which is. (*Pensées sans ordre*, p. 49)

St John does not say: we shall be happy because we see God; but: we shall be like God, because we shall see him as he is.

We shall be pure good.

We shall no longer exist. But in that nothingness which is at the limit of good we shall be more real than at any moment of our earthly life. Whereas the nothingness which is at the limit of evil is without reality.

Reality and existence are two things, not one. (FLN, p. 311)

If we put obedience to God above everything else, unreservedly, with the following thought: 'Suppose God is real, then our gain is total – even though we fall into nothingness at the moment of death; suppose the word 'God' stands only for illusions, then we have still lost nothing because on this assumption there is absolutely nothing good, and consequently nothing to lose; we have even gained, through being in accord with truth, because we have left aside the illusory goods which exist but are not good for the sake of something which (on this assumption) does not exist but which, if it did exist, would be the only good . . .'

If one follows this rule of life, then no revelation at the

moment of death can cause any regrets; because if chance or the devil govern all worlds we would still have no regrets for having lived this way.

That is greatly preferable to Pascal's wager.

If God should be an illusion from the point of view of existence, he is the sole reality from the point of view of the good. I know that for certain, because it is a definition. 'God is the good' is as certain as 'I am'. I am in accord with the truth if I wrench my desire away from everything which is not a good, so as to direct it solely towards the good, without knowing whether the good exists or not.

When once all my desire is directed towards the good, what other good have I to expect? I now possess all the good. That is what it is to possess all the good. How absurd to imagine any other happiness!

For the privilege of finding myself before I die in a state perfectly similar to Christ's when he said, on the cross: 'My God, why hast thou forsaken me?' – for that privilege I would willingly renounce everything that is called paradise.

Because all his desire was entirely directed towards God, and therefore he perfectly possessed God.

He was enduring almost infernal suffering, but what does that detail matter?

It is in respect of false goods that desire and possession are different things; for the true good, there is no difference.

Therefore, God exists because I desire him; that is as certain as my existence. (FLN, p. 157)

d. The desire for good

All I can do is to desire the good. But whereas all other desires are sometimes effective and sometimes not, according to circumstances, this one desire is always effective. The reason is that, whereas the desire for gold is not the same thing as gold, the desire for good is itself a good.

If the day comes when all the desire in my soul is detached from the things of this world and directed wholly and exclusively towards the good, then on that day I shall possess the sovereign good.

Will it be said that I shall be left without an object of

desire? No, because desiring in itself will be my good. Then will it be said that I shall still have something left to desire? No, because I shall possess the object of my desire. Desire itself will be my treasure. (FLN, p. 316)

Once one has recognized God as the supreme and real good, eternally satisfied by himself, that is enough. One may suppose not only that he neither rewards nor punishes his creatures, but even that he ignores their efforts to obey him, their lapses, or their revolts. One will desire nevertheless, more than anything else, to obey him – with a desire stronger than hunger, thirst, the sensual fire, or the craving for respite in the midst of physical torture. At the same time, everything will appear unimportant, including one's own possession of God, in the face of the certainty that he possesses himself eternally and perfectly.

All the desire which nature has placed in the human soul and attached to food, drink, rest, physical comfort, the pleasures of the eye and ear, and other human beings, should be detached from those things and directed exclusively towards obedience to God. (FLN, p. 136)

I find myself in this world with my desire attached to things which are not real goods, things which are neither good nor bad. I must wrench it away from them, but that makes one bleed.

It is not surprising that desire should be different from possession so long as desire is attached to those things, because what it needs is something good, and they are not good.

So soon as it detaches itself and turns towards the good, desire is possession.

But this does not happen for all the soul's desire at the same time. At first only for an infinitesimal part.

Yet this grain of desire which is possession is stronger than all the rest of desire, which is empty.

If I desire only to desire the good, then in desiring the good my desire is fulfilled to overflowing.

It is no more difficult than that.

And I have no need to imagine something behind this word. On the contrary, the object of my desire must be nothing but the reality, completely unknown to me, which is behind the word.

I desire exclusively the good (I mean, that is what I ought to do), but I know that I know absolutely nothing about the good which I exclusively desire, except its name. And yet my desire is perfectly fulfilled, and I need absolutely nothing else.

The secret of salvation is so simple that it escapes the intelligence by its simplicity. It is like a play on words. (FLN, pp. 157, 158)

Essence of faith: It is impossible really to desire the good and not obtain it.

Or reciprocally: anything which it is possible really to desire without obtaining it is not really the good.

It is impossible to receive the good when one has not desired it. (FLN, p. 142)

There is something mysterious in the universe which is in complicity with those who desire nothing but the good. (FLN, p. 355)

Love of truth is not a correct form of expression. Truth is not an object of love. It is not an object at all. What one loves is something which exists, which one thinks on, and which may hence be an occasion for truth or error. A truth is always the truth with reference to something. Truth is the radiant manifestation of reality. Truth is not the object of love but reality. To desire truth is to desire direct contact with a piece of reality. To desire contact with a piece of reality is to love. We desire truth only in order to love in truth. We desire to know the truth about what we love. Instead of talking about love of truth, it would be better to talk about the spirit of truth in love. (*The Need for Roots*, p. 242)

e. Creation, existence and non-being

God abandons our whole entire being – flesh, blood, sensibility, intelligence, love – to the pitiless necessity of matter and the cruelty of the devil, except for the eternal and supernatural part of the soul.

The Creation is an abandonment. In creating what is other than himself, God necessarily abandoned it. He only keeps under his care the part of Creation which is himself – the uncreated part of every creature. That is the life, the Light, the Word; it is the presence here below of God's only Son.

It is sufficient if we consent to this ordering of things.

How can this consent be united with compassion? How is it an act of unique love, when it seems irreconcilable with love? Wisdom, teach me this.

God is absent from the world, except in the existence in this world of those in whom His love is alive. Therefore they ought to be present in the world through compassion. Their compassion is the visible presence of God here below.

When we are lacking in compassion we make a violent separation between a creature and God.

Through compassion we can put the created, temporal part of a creature in communication with God.

It is a marvel analogous to the act of creating itself. (FLN, p. 103)

Because he is the creator, God is not all-powerful. Creation is abdication. But he is all-powerful in this sense, that his abdication is voluntary. He knows its effects, and wills them.

He wills to give his bread to whoever asks for it, but only to him who asks, and only his bread. He has abandoned the whole of our being, except for that part of our soul which dwells, like him, in the heavens. Christ himself did not know this truth until he was on the Cross.

The power of God here below, compared to that of the Prince of this world, is something infinitely small.

God has abandoned God.

God has emptied himself. This means that both the Creation and the Incarnation are included with the Passion. (FLN, p. 120)

God himself cannot prevent what has happened from having happened. What better proof that the creation is an abdication?

What greater abdication of God than is represented by time?

We are abandoned in time.

Creation and original sin are only two aspects, which are different for us, of a single act of abdication by God. And the Incarnation, the Passion, are also aspects of this act.

God emptied himself of his divinity and filled us with a false divinity. Let us empty ourselves of it. This act is the purpose of the act by which we were created.

At this very moment God, by his creative will, is maintaining me in existence, in order that I may renounce it. (FLN, p. 140)

God's attributes do not overflow one another.

They all have the same limit, the abdication which is God's creative act.

We abolish that limit by abdicating in our turn from our existence as creatures. (FLN, p. 125)

God and creation are One; God and creation are infinitely distant from each other: this fundamental contradiction is reflected in that between the necessary and the good. To feel this distance means a spiritual quartering, it means crucifixion. (*Notebooks*, Vol. II, p. 400)

God asked us 'do you want to be created?' and we answered yes. He still asks us at every moment, and at every moment we answer yes. Except for a few whose soul is split in two; while nearly their whole soul answers yes, there is one point in it which wears itself out in beseeching: no, no, no! This point grows larger as it cries, and becomes a patch which eventually spreads throughout the soul. (FLN, p. 211)

Two unconditional truths which neither my sins nor my afflictions have altered, do alter, or can ever alter in any way:

The Good is real.

The entire universe and all its parts, including myself, are perfectly and exclusively obedient to the Good.

God is our only debtor; for no created thing can harm us or deprive us of any good except with his permission. To forgive him his debt is to recognize that he always and unceasingly gives us as much good as we consent to receive.

God's great crime against us is to have created us, is the fact of our existence. And our existence is our great crime against God. When we forgive God for our existence, he forgives us for existing.

We have to know that we are nothing, that the impression of being somebody is an illusion, and we have to carry submission to the point of consenting, not only to be nothing, but at the same time to be under the illusion of being something. Then the wheel of obedience has turned full circle; we have returned, in appearance, to the place where we began, the place of those who do not love God. And then God pardons us for existing.

God pardons us for existing so soon as we are willing to consent to exist only in so far as God wills our existence. (FLN, p. 263)

God created me as a non-being which has the appearance of existing, in order that through love I should renounce this apparent existence and be annihilated by the plenitude of being. (FLN, p. 96)

God created me as a non-being which has the appearance of existing, in order that through love I should renounce what I think is my existence and so emerge from non-being. Then there is no 'I'. The 'I' belongs to non-being. But I have not the right to know this. If I knew it, where would be the renunciation? I shall never know it. (FLN, pp. 96, 97)

Really to die, in the moral sense, means consenting to submit to everything whatsoever that chance may bring. Because chance can deprive me of everything that I call 'I'.

To consent to being a creature and nothing else. It is like consenting to lose one's whole existence.

We are nothing but creatures. But to consent to be nothing but that is like consenting to be nothing. Without our knowing it, this being which God has given us is non-being. If we desire non-being, we have it and all we have to do is to be aware of the fact.

Our sin consists in wanting to be, and our punishment is that we believe we possess being. Expiation consists in desiring to cease to be; and salvation consists for us in perceiving that we are not.

Adam made us believe that we had being; Christ showed us that we are non-beings.

To teach us that we are non-beings, God made himself non-being.

For God, sacrifice consists in letting a man believe that he has being. For a man, sacrifice consists in recognizing that he is non-being.

God entrusts to evil the work of teaching us that we are not.

The desire of creatures to be, and their illusion that they are, stirs up evil; and evil teaches them that they are not. God takes no part in this elementary stage of teaching.

Those who have fully recognized their own non-being have passed over to God's side. So far from teaching other creatures that they are non-being, they treat them on the fictitious assumption that they possess being.

Creation is a fiction of God's.

The quantity of evil in the world is precisely equal to the necessary amount of punishment. But it strikes haphazardly.

To suffer evil is the only way of destroying it.

No action destroys evil, but only the apparently useless and perfectly patient suffering of it.

The imaginary existence of thinking creatures who believe they exist is what rebounds in the form of evil. Evil is illusory, and whoever has escaped from the illusion is released from all evil. Moreover, evil is an illusion which can itself in certain conditions stimulate a man to escape from illusion.

Hell consists in perceiving that one does not exist and refusing to consent to this fact.

Purity attracts evil, which rushes to it like moths to a flame, to be destroyed.

Everything has to pass through the fire. But those who have become flame are at home in the fire. But in order to become fire it is necessary to have passed through hell. (FLN, pp. 217, 218)

f. Necessity, the condition of the cosmos

This sensible universe in which we find ourselves has no other reality than that of necessity; and necessity is a combination of relations which fade away as soon as they are not sustained by a pure and lofty concentration on the part of the mind. This universe around us is made up of mind materially present in our flesh. (*The Need for Roots*, p. 279)

The operation of the intellect in scientific study makes sovereign necessity over matter appear to the mind as a network of relations which are immaterial and without force. Necessity can only be perfectly conceived so long as such relations appear as absolutely immaterial. They are then only present to the understanding as a result of a pure and lofty concentration emanating from a part of the mind not subjected to force. The part of the human mind that is subjected to force is that part which finds itself under the sway of needs. One has to forget entirely all about needs in order to conceive the relations in their immaterial purity. If one manages to do this, one realizes the play of forces in accordance with which the satisfaction of needs is granted or refused. (*The Need for Roots*, p. 277)

The order of the world is the same as the beauty of the world. All that differs is the type of concentration demanded, according to whether one tries to conceive the necessary relations which go to make it up or to contemplate its splendour.

It is one and the same thing, which with respect to God is eternal Wisdom; with respect to the universe, perfect obedience; with respect to our love, beauty; with respect to our intelligence, balance of necessary relations; with respect to our flesh, brute force. (*The Need for Roots*, p. 281)

Necessity: ensemble of laws of variation which are determined by fixed and invariant ratios. (FLN, p. 88)

Necessity – freedom; obedience is their unity.
Necessity, obedience of matter to God. (FLN, p. 90)

The universe, compact mass of obedience with luminous points. Everything is beautiful. (FLN, p. 90)

The Pythagoreans said, not the union of the limited and the limitless, but what is much more beautiful: the union of that which limits and the non-limited. That which limits is God. God who says to the sea: Hitherto shalt thou come, but no further ... . That which is unlimited has no existence except in receiving a limit from outside. All that exists here below is similarly constituted; not only all material realities but all the psychological realities in ourselves and in others as well. (*Intimations of Christianity*, p. 100)

The recognition of might as an absolutely sovereign thing in all of nature, including the natural part of the human soul, with all the thoughts and all the feelings the soul contains, and at the same time as an absolutely detestable thing; this is the innate grandeur of Greece. Today one sees many people who honour might above all, whether they give it that name or other names possessed of a more agreeable sound. . . . For to know, not abstractly but with the whole soul, that all in nature, including psychological nature, is under the dominance of a force as brutal, as pitilessly directed downward as gravity, such a knowledge glues, so to speak, the soul to prayer like a prisoner who, when he is able, remains glued to the window of his cell, or like a fly stays stuck to the bottom of a bottle by the force of its urge toward the light. (*Intimations of Christianity*, p. 116)

For us, matter is simply what is subjected to necessity. We know nothing else about it. Necessity is constituted for us by the quantitative laws of variation in the appearances. (*Intimations of Christianity*, p. 179)

Necessity is an enemy for man as long as he thinks in the first person. (*Intimations of Christianity*, p. 180)

In the universe, man experiences necessity only so far as it is at once an obstacle and a condition of accomplishing his will. (*Intimations of Christianity*, p. 181)

So long as we think in the first person, we see necessity from below, from inside, it encloses us on all sides as the surface of the earth and the arc of the sky. From the time we renounce thinking in the first person, by consent to necessity, we see it from outside, beneath us for we have passed to God's side. The side which it turned to us before, and still presents to almost the whole of our being, the natural part of ourselves, is brute domination. The side which it presents after this operation, to the fragment of our mind which has passed to the other side, is pure obedience. We have become sons of the home, and we love the docility of this slave, necessity, which at first we took for a master. (*Intimations of Christianity*, pp. 186, 187)

At the end of such meditations, one reaches an extremely simple view of the universe. God has created, that is, not that he has produced something outside himself, but that he has withdrawn himself, permitting a part of being to be other than God. To this divine renunciation, the renunciation of creation responds, that is to say, obedience, responds. The whole universe is a compact mass of obedience. This compact mass is sprinkled with points of light. Each one of these points is the supernatural part of the soul of a reasonable creature who loves God and who consents to obey. The rest of the soul is held in the compact mass. The beings gifted with reason who do not love God are only fragments of the compact and obscure mass. They also are wholly obedient but only in the manner of a falling stone. Their soul also is matter, psychic matter, humbled to a mechanism as rigorous as that of gravity. Even their belief in their own free arbitration, the illusions of their pride, their defiance, their revolts, are all simply phenomena as rigorously determined as the refraction of light. Considered thus, as inert matter, the worst criminals make up a part of the order of the world and therefore of the beauty of the world. Everything obeys God, therefore everything is perfect beauty. To know that, to know it really, is to be perfect as the heavenly Father is perfect. (*Intimations of Christianity*, pp. 193, 194)

If one believes that God has created in order to be loved, and that he cannot create anything which is God, and further that he cannot be loved by anything which is not God, he is then brought up against a contradiction. The contradiction contains in itself Necessity. On the other hand, every contradiction resolves itself through the process of becoming. God has created a finite being, which says 'I', which is unable to love God. Through the action of grace the 'I' little by little disappears, and God loves himself by way of the creature, which empties itself, becomes nothing. When it has disappeared . . . he goes on creating more creatures and helping them to re-create themselves.

Time arises out of the state of becoming implied by this contradiction.

The necessity contained in this contradiction represents the whole of Necessity in a nutshell. (*Notebooks*, Vol. I, pp. 330,

. . . How widely separated the essence of the necessary is from that of the good. (*Notebooks*, Vol. II, p. 379)

The distance between the necessary and the good is the selfsame distance separating the creature from the creator. – God, with respect to creation, in so far as perfectly present and in so far as perfectly absent. (*Notebooks*, Vol. II, p. 379)

The apparent absence of God in this world is the actual reality of God. The same is true for everything. Whatever is in appearance is unreality.

Appearance possesses the fulness of reality, but as appearance only. As anything other than appearance it constitutes error.

This world, in so far as it is completely empty of God, is God himself.

Necessity, in so far as it is absolutely other than Good, is Good itself.

That is why any form of consolation in affliction draws us away from love and truth.

Therein lies the greatest of all mysteries. When we can lay our finger on it, then we are safe. (*Notebooks*, Vol. II, p. 424)

g. Work

In crops and vines all the energy of the sun is captured and concentrated through the medium of chlorophyll. By this means the energy of the sun itself enters men and gives them life . . .

The peasant plays his part in this process . . .

Death and labour are things of necessity and not of choice. The world only gives itself to man in the form of food and warmth if man gives himself in the form of labour. Consent to suffer death, when death is there and seen in all its nakedness, consitutes a final, sudden, wrenching away from what each calls 'I'. Consent to perform labour is of a less violent nature. But where it is absolute it is renewed each morning throughout the entire length of human existence, day after day, and each day it lasts until the evening, and it starts again on the following day, and this goes on often until death. Each morning the labourer consents to perform his labour for that day, and for the rest of his life.

He exhausts himself by work in order that he may eat, and he eats in order that he may have the strength to work, and after a year of toil, everything is as it was when he began. Only if his labour is illumined by the light of eternity will the monotony become bearable.

A labourer burns up his own flesh and transforms it into energy like a machine burning coal. (He) transforms his own flesh and blood into the fruits of his labour, food and wine . . . Manual labour is either a degrading servitude or a sacrifice.

(Pensées sans ordre, pp. 19, 20, 25, 29)

Nothing is worse than a mixture of monotony and the unpredictable. In the factory new work is sprung upon you in the form of an order which must be obeyed immediately. If only the boss would say a week in advance: 'You're going to be put on crank-arms for two days, and then drilling', you would still have to obey, but at least it would be possible to hold the immediate future in your imagination, to possess it. But it's not like that. At any moment from clocking in to clocking out, a new order may come. (*La condition ouvrière*, p. 332)

h. False religion, the wrong relation between necessity and good

Religion in so far as it is a source of consolation is a hindrance to true faith. (*Notebooks*, Vol. I, p. 238)

The outstanding atheistic idea is the idea of progress, which is the negation of experimental ontological proof, and implies that what is of indifferent quality can of itself produce what is of the best quality. (*Notebooks*, Vol. II, p. 435)

The service of the false God (of the Social Beast in whatever form it may be) purifies evil by eliminating the horror of it. Nothing seems – or at any rate ought any longer to seem – evil to him who serves the false God, except lapses in the performance of his service. The service of the true God allows the horror of evil to subsist, and even renders it more intense. Whilst one has a horror of this evil, at the same time one loves it as emanating from the will of God.

Idolatry is due to the fact that, while athirst for absolute good, one is not in possession of supernatural attention; and one has not the patience to let it grow. (*Notebooks*, Vol. II, pp. 504, 505)

Totalitarianism is an ersatz form of Christianity.

Christianity became a totalitarian, conquering and destroying agent because it failed to develop the notion of the absence and non-action of God here below. (*Notebooks*, Vol. II, p. 505)

There are two forms of good, of the same denomination, but radically different from each other : one which is the opposite of evil, and one which is the absolute – the absolute which cannot be anything but the good. The absolute has no opposite. The relative is not the opposite of the absolute; it is derived from it through a non-commutative relationship. What we want is the absolute good. What is within our reach is the good which is correlated to evil. We mistakenly take it for what we want, like the prince who sets about making love to the maid instead of the mistress. The mistake is due to the clothes. It is the social element which sheds the colour of the absolute over the relative. Even love, even greediness, come under the social influence (fashion . . .). The remedy is the idea of relationship. Relationship breaks violently away from the social. It is the monopoly of the individual. Social forms of good are conventionally accepted forms of good. Social convention, the convenience of social conventions in general, or more precisely, the ordering of the City, the Law, constitutes the fire, the actual light, albeit an earthly one, which casts the shadows. Particular conventions, such as royalty, are fabricated objects. We look for the shadows of conventions. We are chained down in the midst of society. Society is the Cave. The way out is solitude. (*Notebooks*, Vol. II, pp. 592, 593)

God can become a piece of bread, a stone, a tree, a lamb, a man. But he cannot become a people. No people can become an incarnation of God.

The Devil is the collective. (Which in Durkheim is the divinity.) This is clearly indicated in the Apocalypse by that beast which is so obviously the Great Beast of Plato.

Pride is the Devil's characteristic attribute. And pride is a social thing. . . . Pride is the instinct of social conservation. Humility is the acceptance of social death.

I am more and more afraid that in the Apocalypse the False Prophet represents, in the author's mind, the Church. (FLN, p. 304)

Only an order from God is eternal.

Only the unconditional leads to God.

(A mass 'offered for . . .', a prayer, or a suffering, 'offered for . . .', are not contacts with God.)

The unconditioned is contact with God. Everything that is conditioned is of this world.

(Ex. Jacob: If . . . if . . . if . . . *then* shall the Lord be my God.)[1] (FLN, p. 127)

All attempts to discover in the structure of the universe evidence of the benevolent intentions of the owner of it are without any exception on the same level as that remark of Bernardin de Saint-Pierre's on the subject of melons and meals *en famille*.[2] There is in all these attempts the same basic absurdity which we find in historical considerations concerning the effects of the Incarnation. The good which it is given to Man to observe in the universe is finite, limited. To endeavour to discern therein evidence of divine action is to turn God himself into a finite, a limited good. It is a blasphemy. (*The Need for Roots*, p. 268)

When the notion of Providence is made to enter private

---

[1] *Genesis* 28:20-1.
[2] . . . meals *'en famille'*: Bernardin de Saint-Pierre was so convinced of the essential harmony in Nature, that he thought he saw a divine significance in the fact that melons indicate from the outside their division into slices, which was an unmistakable sign that they were meant to be eaten *en famille*.

life, the result is no less comical. If lightning falls within an inch of somebody without touching him, he often thinks it is Providence which has preserved him. Those who happen to be a mile away from that spot have no idea that they owe their lives to an intervention on the part of God. Apparently, when the mechanism of the universe is on the point of causing the death of any human being, God asks himself whether it pleases him or not to save the creature's life, and if he decides it does he exerts an imperceptible pressure on the mechanism. He can well change the course of the lightning by an inch in order to save a life, but not by a mile, still less prevent it from falling purely and simply. Evidently people must reason in this fashion; otherwise they would say to themselves that Providence intervenes in order to prevent us from being killed by lightning at every moment of our lives, to the same extent as at the moment when it falls an inch away from us. The only time when it doesn't intervene to prevent the lightning killing such-and-such a human being is the very instant when the lightning kills him, if that indeed occurs. Everything which doesn't happen is prevented from happening by God to the same extent. Everything which happens is permitted to happen by God to the same extent.

The ridiculous conception of Providence as being a personal and particular intervention on the part of God for certain particular ends is incompatible with true faith. But it is not a manifest incompatibility. It is incompatible with the scientific conception of the world; and in this case the incompatibility is manifest. Christians who, under the influence of education and surroundings, carry within them this conception of Providence, also carry within them the scientific conception of the world, and that divides their minds into two water-tight compartments: one for the scientific conception of the world, the other for the conception of the world as being a field in which God's personal Providence is exercised. This makes it impossible for them really to think either the one or the other. The second one, moreover, will not bear serious scrutiny. Unbelievers, not being inhibited by any motives of reverence, detect easily enough the ridiculous aspect of this personal and particular form of Providence, and religious faith itself is, on account of it, made to seem ridiculous in their eyes. (*The Need for Roots*, pp. 269, 270)

It is, above all, the fundamental contradiction, that between the good and necessity, or its equivalent, that between justice and force, whose use constitutes a criterion. As Plato said, an infinite distance separates the good from necessity. They have nothing in common. They are totally other. Although we are forced to assign them a unity, this unity is a mystery; it remains for us a secret. The genuine religious life is the contemplation of this unknown unity.

The manufacture of a fictitious, mistaken equivalent of this unity, brought within the grasp of the human faculties, is at the bottom of the inferior forms of the religious life. To every genuine form of the religious life there corresponds an inferior form, which is based to all appearances on the same doctrine, but has no understanding of it. But the converse is not true. There are ways of thinking that are compatible only with a religious life of inferior quality.

In this respect the whole of materialism, in so far as it attributes to matter the automatic manufacture of the good, is to be classed among the inferior forms of the religious life. This is demonstrated even in the case of the bourgeois economists of the nineteenth century, the apostles of. liberalism, who adopt a truly religious accent when they talk about production. It is demonstrated to a far greater degree still in the case of Marxism. Marxism is a fully-fledged religion, in the impurest sense of the word. In particular it shares in common with all inferior forms of the religious life the fact of having been continually used, according to Marx's perfectly accurate expression, as an opium of the people. (*Oppression and Liberty*, p. 174)

i. True religion

M. Pouget. 'The science of religions has not yet begun.' Assuredly.

It is the science of the supernatural in its various manifestations through the various human societies.

Christians and non-Christians are alike incapable of understanding this.

(That there were supernatural manifestations before Christ is admitted. Why not then among all peoples? Which would imply in all religions, for they are all prior to Christ, except for the Mohammedan religion, which is strongly contaminated by Christianity.) (*Notebooks*, Vol. I, p. 226)

Each religion is alone true, that is to say, that at the moment we are thinking on it we must bring as much attention to bear on it as if there were nothing else; in the same way, each landscape, each picture, each poem, etc. is alone beautiful. A 'synthesis' of religions implies a lower quality of attention. (*Notebooks*, Vol. I, p. 228)

We should conceive the identity of the various traditions, not by reconciling them through what they have in common, but by grasping the essence of what is specific in each. For this essence is one and the same. (*Notebooks*, Vol. II, p. 502)

There are idiots who speak of syncretism in connection with Plato. But there is no need to syncretize what is all one thing. In Thales, Anaximander, Heraclitus, Socrates, Pythagoras, there is the same doctrine, the single Greek doctrine, expressed through different temperaments. (FLN, p. 351)

I believe that one identical thought is to be found – expressed very precisely and with only very slight differences of modality – in the ancient mythologies; in the philosophies of Pherekydes, Thales, Anaximander, Heraclitus, Pythagoras, Plato, and the Greek Stoics; in Greek poetry of the great age; in universal folklore; in the Upanishads and the Bhagavad Gita; in the Chinese Taoist writings and in certain currents of Buddhism; in what remains of the sacred writings of Egypt; in the dogmas of the Christian faith and in the writings of the greatest Christian mystics, especially St John of the Cross; and in certain heresies, especially the Cathar and Manichean tradition. I believe that this thought is the truth, and that it requires today a modern and Western form of expression. That is to say, it requires to be expressed through the only approximately good thing we can call our own, namely science. (Letter to Jean Wahl, *Seventy Letters*, p. 159, translated from the magazine *Deucalion*, Gallimard)

It is from this thought that Christianity issued; but only the

Gnostics, Manicheans, and Cathars seem to have kept really faithful to it. They alone really escaped the coarseness of mind and baseness of heart which were disseminated over vast territories by the Roman domination and which still, today, compose the atmosphere of Europe.

There is something more in the Manicheans than in antiquity, or at least than in antiquity as known to us; there are some magnificent conceptions, such as the descent of divinity among men and the rending of the spirit and its dispersal throughout matter. But what above all makes the fact of Catharism a sort of miracle is that it was a religion and not simply a philosophy. I mean that around Toulouse in the 12th century the highest thought dwelt within a whole human environment and not only in the minds of a certain number of individuals. That, it seems to me, is the sole difference between philosophy and religion, so long as religion is something not dogmatic.

No thought attains to its fullest existence unless it is incarnated in a human environment, and by environment I mean something open to the world around, something which is steeped in the surrounding society and is in contact with the whole of it, and not simply a closed circle of disciples around a master. (Letter to Déodat Roché, *Seventy Letters*, pp. 130, 131)

A life in which the supernatural truths would be read in every kind of work, in every act of labour, in all festivals, in all hierarchical social relations, in all art, in all science, in all philosophy. (FLN, p. 173)

Science, art and religion are connected together through the notion of *order of the world*, which we have completely lost. (*Notebooks*, Vol. I, p. 248)

Study of a religion from the historical, sociological, etc. angles : finding out the *conditions of existence* – which reserves the problem as to the value of the revelation. (*Notebooks*, Vol. I, p. 243)

By saying that the Catholic religion is true and the other religions false, one does an injustice not only to the other religious traditions but to the Catholic faith itself, by placing it on the level of those things which can be affirmed or denied. (*Notebooks*, Vol. I, p. 242)

Brute force is not sovereign in this world. It is by nature blind and indeterminate. What is sovereign in this world is determinateness, limit. Eternal wisdom imprisons this universe in a network, a web of determinations. The universe accepts passively. The brute force of matter, which appears to us sovereign, is nothing else in reality but perfect obedience.

That is the guarantee accorded to Man, the Ark of the Covenant, the Covenant, the visible and palpable promise here below, the sure basis of hope. That is the truth which bites at our hearts every time we are penetrated by the beauty of the world. That is the truth which bursts forth in matchless accents of joy in the beautiful and pure parts of the Old Testament, in Greece among the Pythagoreans and all the sages, in China with Lao-Tse, in the Hindu scriptures, in Egyptian remains. It lies perhaps hidden in innumerable myths and tales. It will appear to us, before our very eyes, clothed in our own knowledge, if one day God opens our eyes, as he did Hagar's. (*The Need for Roots*, p. 272)

The Gospel contains a conception of human life, not a theology. (FLN, p. 147)

Our life is nothing but impossibility, absurdity. Each thing that we desire is in contradiction with the conditions or the consequences attaching to that thing; each assertion that we make implies the contrary assertion; all our feelings are mixed up with their opposites. The reason is that we are made up of contradiction, since we are creatures, and at the same time God, and at the same time infinitely other than God.

Contradiction alone makes us experience the fact that we are not All. Contradiction is our wretchedness, and the feeling of our wretchedness is the feeling of reality. For our wretchedness is not something that we concoct. It is something truly real. That is why we must love it. All the rest is imaginary.

In order to be just, one must be naked and dead -- without imagination. That is why the ideal of justice has to be naked and dead. The Cross alone is not exposed to an imaginary imitation.

So that we may feel the distance between us and God, God has to be a crucified slave. For we can only feel this distance looking downwards. It is very much easier to place oneself in imagination in the position of God the Creator than it is in that of Christ crucified.

It is not by eating the fruit of a certain tree, as Adam thought, that one becomes the equal of God, but by going the way of the Cross.

It is obvious that the pure ideal of justice held up for imitation must possess nothing of what circumstances can give or take away. It must only have in the way of circumstances that which we cannot possibly wish for. In this way the resemblance to it that we desire to acquire has nothing whatever to do with the circumstances. If this ideal were a just king, one would desire to be king, not to be just.

One can give oneself in imagination whatever one desires. One cannot desire the Cross. By contemplating our wretchedness in Christ, we learn to love it.

The correlation of contraries that is representable to the mind is an image of the transcendent correlation of contradictories.

Correlations of contraries are like a ladder. Each of them raises us to a higher level where resides the connexion which unifies the contraries; until we reach a spot where we have to think of the contraries together, but where we are denied access to the level at which they are linked together. This forms the last rung of the ladder. Once arrived there, we can climb no further; we have only to look up, wait and love. And God descends.

This is so both in the case of thought and in that of action, in the case of truth as in that of good.

Symmetrical solid bodies and the fourth dimension are an image of this.

A man inspired by God is a man who has ways of behaving, thoughts and feelings which are linked together by a link impossible to define. (*Notebooks*, Vol. II, pp. 411, 412)

I feel an ever increasing sense of devastation, both in my intellect and in the centre of my heart, at my inability to think with truth at the same time about the affliction of men, the perfection of God, and the link between the two. (Letter to Maurice Schumann, *Seventy Letters*, p. 178, translated from *Ecrits de Londres*, Gallimard)

j. Theory of the Sacraments

Human nature is so arranged that a desire of the soul has no reality within the soul until it has passed through the body by means of actions, movements and attitudes. Until then it is like a ghost. It has no effect on the soul.

On this arrangement is based the possibility of a certain self-control by the exercise of the will, through the natural link between the will and the muscles.

But if the exercise of the will can, and that only to a limited extent, prevent the soul from falling into evil, it cannot of itself increase in the soul the proportion of good to evil.

If you don't have in your wallet all the money that you require, you have to obtain more from a bank. You will not provide it for yourself, because you don't have it.

No matter what effort we make, we cannot acquire for ourselves the good which is not in us. We can only receive it.

We can receive it without the slightest doubt, on just one condition. That condition is desire. But not desire for a partial good.

Only the desire which is focused directly upon pure, perfect, total and absolute good can produce in the soul more good than was there before. When a soul is in this state of desire, its progress is proportional to the intensity of the desire and to the pressures of time.

But any desire has to be real to be effective. Similarly, the desire for absolute good is effective inasmuch as, and only inasmuch as, it is real.

If bodily movements and attitudes can only draw their objects from this world, how can this desire pass through the body into the state of reality?

It is impossible.

But wherever it is certain that something essential for salvation is impossible, it is also certain that there really exists a supernatural possibility.

In everything that concerns absolute good and contact with it, the proof by perfection (sometimes wrongly called ontological) is not only a valid proof, but is the only valid one. It follows directly from the very notion of good. It is for good what geometrical demonstration is for necessity.

In order that the desire for absolute good should pass through the body there must be an object from this world which can be absolute good in terms of the flesh, as a symbol and by agreement.

That it should be absolute good in terms of the flesh does not mean that it is a good of the flesh. It is the absolute spiritual good in terms of the flesh.

An agreement concerning things of this world can be concluded and ratified between men, or between a man and himself.

An agreement concerning absolute good can only be ratified by God.

(This idea of divine ratification is what, in the canon of the mass, immediately precedes the Consecration.)

Divine ratification necessarily implies a direct revelation from God, and perhaps even Incarnation.

Only things which have been established by God as symbols can serve as such.

Through an agreement established by God between himself and men, a piece of bread signifies the person of Christ. Consequently, since an agreement ratified by God is infinitely more real than matter, its reality as bread, though remaining, is reduced to the level of appearance by comparison with the infinitely greater reality of what it signifies.

In agreements established between men, an object's symbolic reality is less than its material reality. The contrary is the case with agreements established by God. The divine significance encroaches infinitely further upon matter, in terms of their respective degrees of reality, than the human significance is encroached upon by matter.

If you believe that contact with the piece of bread is contact with God, in that case in the contact with bread the desire for contact with God, which was only an impulse, passes the test of reality.

Because of this same fact, and because in these matters

desiring is the one precondition for receiving, there is a real contact between the soul and God.

With things of this world belief produces illusion. It is only with respect to divine things that belief has the virtue of producing something real, through the operation of desire, at the moment when a soul keeps its desire and attention directed towards God. Belief which produces something real is called faith.

Grace is at the same time both the most external and the most internal thing to us. The good only comes to us from without, but it is only the good to which we consent that penetrates us, and consent is not real except at the moment when the body by a gesture makes it so.

We cannot transform ourselves. We can only be transformed, and then only if we desire the good. A fragment of matter does not have the power to change us. But if we believe that it does have it through God's will, and for that reason we take it into ourselves, then we really do achieve a receptivity to the desired transformation, which consequently comes upon the soul from the height of heaven. In that way the fragment of matter did have the power attributed to it.

The sacrament is an arrangement which irreproachably and perfectly corresponds to the twofold operation of grace, as something received both passively and with active consent, and to the relation between the reflective and physical aspects of man.

For belief in the supernatural mechanism of the sacrament to have this power there is a double condition.

First, the object of desire must be none other than the unique, pure, perfect, complete, absolute and, for us, inconceivable good. Plenty of people apply the word God as a courtesy title to some conception that they have fabricated or that their social milieu has provided. There are many conceptions of this kind. They more or less resemble the true God, but the soul can think them without actually looking outside the world at all. In that case thought, though apparently occupied with God, remains in this world, and belief, according to the world's own canons, produces illusion and not truth.

However, this is not a hopeless state, since the names of God and Christ have such a power in themselves that they can in time lead the soul out of it and into truth.

The second condition is that the belief in a certain identity between the piece of bread and God should have penetrated one's whole being to the point of infecting, not the intelligence, which has no place at this stage, but all the other parts of the soul, imagination, sensitivity, almost the flesh itself.

When these two conditions exist, and when the approaching contact with the bread is about to subject desire to the test of reality, something really happens in the soul.

As long as a desire has no contact with reality, it does not become a centre of conflict in the soul. For example, if a man sincerely desires to face death fighting for his country, but is not in a position to take any step towards that goal, if for example he is half-paralysed, his desire will not be brought into tension in his soul with the fear of death.

If a man is in a position either to go to fight or to keep away, if he decides to go, and takes steps in this direction and succeeds and is under fire, and is sent on an extremely dangerous mission and is killed; it is almost certain that at some moment in this progress of duty, the fear of death will arise in his soul and be confronted. That moment could occur at any stage, depending on temperament and quality of imagination. Only at the arrival of this moment has the desire to risk death become real.

It is the same with the desire for contact with God. Until it is real, it leaves the soul undisturbed.

But when the conditions for a true sacrament exist, and when that sacrament is about to take place, then the soul is divided.

One part of it, of which we may not even be aware for the moment, aspires after the sacrament; that is the portion of truth in the soul; for 'he who does what is true comes to the light.'

But all that is mediocre in the soul revolts at the sacrament, showing far more hatred and fear than even an animal's body shows when it recoils before its killer. For 'everyone who does what is mediocre hates the light.'

Thus begins the separation of the good seed and the tares. Christ said, 'I have not come to bring peace, but a sword.' And Saint Paul, 'For the word of God is living and active, sharper than any two-edged sword, piercing to the division of soul and spirit, of joints and marrow, and discerning the thoughts and intentions of the heart.'

Communion is therefore a journey through fire, which burns and destroys a fragment of the soul's impurities. The next communion destroys another fragment. The amount of evil in the human soul is limited, and the divine fire is inexhaustible. Thus, at the conclusion of the operation, in spite of the worst lapses, arrival at the state of perfection cannot fail, provided that there is no betrayal or deliberate refusal of the good, and that the accident of death does not intervene.

The more real the desire for God, and consequently contact with God through the sacrament, the more violent will be the upheaval of the mediocre part of the soul; an upheaval that is comparable to the recoiling of a living body when it is about to be pushed into fire. According to the particular instance, it takes on the colour mainly of repulsion, or hate, or fear.

When the soul is in such a state that the approach to the sacrament is more painful than the onset of death, it is very near the threshold beyond which martyrdom is easy.

In its desperate effort to survive and escape destruction by fire, the mediocre part of the soul feverishly seeks out arguments, which it borrows from any arsenal that it can find, including theology and all the warnings about not taking the sacrament unworthily.

Provided that these thoughts are not at all heeded by the soul in which they arise, this internal tumult is utterly to be welcomed.

The more violent the internal movement of recoil, revolt and fear, the more certain it is that the sacrament is going to destroy a great deal of evil and carry the soul much nearer to perfection.

'The mustard seed is the smallest of all seeds.'

The imperceptible atom of pure good, which is established in the soul by real movements of desire towards God, is that seed. If it is not snatched away by an intentional betrayal, then inevitably in the course of time there will grow out of it branches in which the birds of the air will make their nests.

Christ said (Mark 4:26-29). 'The kingdom of God is as if a man should scatter seed upon the ground, and should sleep and rise night and day, and the seed should sprout and grow, he knows not how. The earth produces of itself, first the blade, then the ear, then the full grain in the ear. But when the grain is ripe, at once he puts in the sickle, because the harvest has come.'

When the soul has once crossed a threshold through a real contact with pure good – of which internal tumult before the sacrament is perhaps a sure sign – nothing further is asked of it except motionless attention.

Motionless attention does not mean absence of external activity. External activity, as long as it is rigorously imposed by human obligations and particular commandments of God, is one part of this stillness of soul; staying within and going outside both upset the attitude of motionless attention.

One prerequisite for the soul's attentiveness is some activity which is exactly commensurate with what is required, just as, with a child at study, bodily stillness is a prerequisite for concentration.

But, as physical immobility is not the same thing as attention, and is without efficacy in itself, so with the actions prescribed for a soul which has reached this state.

Just as a truly attentive man has no need of self-constraint to arouse in himself attention, but on the contrary, as soon as his thought tackles a problem, naturally and automatically suspends the motions that would disturb it, so from a soul that is in a state of perfect attentiveness the required actions flow spontaneously.

As long as perfection is distant, the actions are frequently mingled with sorrow, pain, tiredness, signs of internal struggling, and lapses, which are often serious; provided, however, that there has been in the soul no intentional betrayal, then there is something about the performance of the actions which is irresistible.

Man cannot do without prescribed actions, but his accessibility to God's love does not depend on his performing them.

'Will any of you, who has a servant ploughing or keeping sheep, say to him when he has come in from the field, "Come at once and sit down at table"? Will he not rather say to him, "Prepare supper for me, and gird yourself and serve me, till I eat and drink; and afterward you shall eat and drink"? Does he thank the servant because he did what was commanded? So you also, when you have done all that is commanded you, say, "We are unworthy servants; we have only done what was our duty." ' (Luke 17:7-10)

The servant who receives the love, gratitude and even the hospitality of his master is not the one who ploughs and reaps. He is another.

This does not mean that there has to be a choice between two ways of serving God. These servants represent two different relationships of the same soul, or again two inseparable parts of the same soul.

The servant who will be loved is the one who stands upright and motionless at the door, in a state of vigil, watchfulness, attentiveness and desire, to open as soon as he hears any knocking.

Nothing will upset his watchful stillness, not to the slightest degree – neither tiredness, nor hunger, nor entreaties, nor friendly invitations, nor injuries, nor the blows or taunts of his fellows, nor the circulation of rumours that his master is dead or displeased with him and intent on harming him.

'Be like men who are waiting for their master to come home from the marriage feast, so that they may open to him at once when he comes and knocks. Blessed are those servants whom the master finds awake when he comes; truly, I say to you, he will gird himself and have them sit at table, and he will come and serve them.'

The state of waiting which is rewarded in this way is usually called patience.

But the Greek word, *hypomoné*, is infinitely more beautiful and has different associations.

It signifies a person who waits without moving, in spite of all the blows from those who try to make him move.

Karpophorousin en hypomoné.

'They will bring forth fruit with patience.'

(*Pensées sans ordre*)

k. 'Last Text'

I believe in God, the Trinity, the Incarnation, Redemption, the Eucharist, and the teachings of the Gospel.

When I say 'I believe' I do not mean that I take over for myself what the Church says on these matters, affirming them as one might affirm empirical facts or geometrical theorems, but that, through love, I hold on to the perfect, unseizable, truth which these mysteries contain, and that I try to open my soul to it so that its light may penetrate into me.

I do not recognize that the Church has any right to limit the operations of intelligence or the illuminations of love in the domain of thought.

I recognize that, as steward of the sacraments and guardian of the sacred texts, she has the task of formulating judgments on a few essential points, but only as a guideline for the faithful.

I do not recognize her right to set up, as being the truth, the commentaries with which she surrounds the mysteries of faith, and much less still the right to use intimidation when, in imposing these commentaries, she exercises her power to deprive people of the sacraments.

For me, in the effort of reflection, a real or apparent disagreement with the Church's teaching is simply a reason for a considerable slowing-down of my thought, and for pushing attentive and scrupulous inquiry as far as it will go, before daring to affirm anything. But that is all.

With that exception, I ponder all the problems raised by the comparative study of religions, their history, the truth enshrined in each one, the relation between religion and the secular forms of the search for truth, indeed the whole of secular life, and the mysterious significance of the texts and traditions of Christianity; all that – without any worry about possible disagreement with the Church's dogmatic teaching.

Knowing myself fallible, and knowing that all the evil that I am cowardly enough to leave in my soul can produce there a proportionate degree of falsehood and error, I doubt in a sense even the things that appear to me most manifestly certain.

But this doubt bears equally on all my thoughts, those which are in agreement with the Church's teaching just as much as those which are in disagreement with it. I hope and assume that I shall continue in this attitude as long as I live.

I am sure that it is not sinful to talk like this. It is by thinking otherwise that I would be committing a crime against my vocation, which demands absolute intellectual honesty.

I can conceive of no advantage, in this world or any other, to be gained from such an attitude. It brings only troubles, moral discomfort and isolation.

Above all it could not be motivated by pride, since there is nothing to flatter pride in a situation in which one is to unbelievers a pathological case, holding to absurd dogmas without the excuse of being subject to some social pressure, and in which one arouses amongst the orthodox the slightly disdainful protective goodwill of him who has arrived for him who is still on the way.

I see therefore no reason for rejecting the feeling in me that I should remain in this attitude out of obedience to God; that if I modified it, I would offend Christ, who said, 'I am the truth.'

On the other hand I have experienced for some time now an intense and ever-increasing desire for communion.

If one looks on the sacraments as a good, if I look on them thus myself, if I desire them, and if I am refused them through no fault of my own, that cannot but be a cruel injustice.

If I, with the attitude in which I am persevering, am granted baptism, in that case a break is being made with a tradition which has lasted at least seventeen centuries.

If that break is just and desirable, if precisely in our time it is found to be of more than vital urgency for the well-being of Christianity – which seems clear to me – for the sake of the Church and the world it should then take place with bursting impact and not with the isolated initiative of one priest performing one obscure and little known baptism.

For this reason and for several others of a similar nature, I have never up to now made a formal request to a priest for baptism.

And I am not doing so now.

Nevertheless I feel the need, not abstract but practical, real and urgent, to know whether, if I did ask, it would be granted or refused.

(The Church would have an easy way of achieving what would be salvation both for herself and for humanity.

She recognizes that the definitions of the Councils have their significance only relative to their historical context.

It is impossible for the non-specialist to know this context, and often even for the specialist because of lack of documents.

It follows that the proclamations of *anathema sit* are only history. They have no present value.

In point of fact they are considered in this way, because no one imposes as a condition for the baptism of an adult that he should have read *The Manual of the Decisions and Formulations of the Councils*. A catechism is not the same thing, since it does not contain all that is technically 'the strict faith', and does contain some things which are not.

Besides, it is impossible to discover by asking priests what is and what isn't 'the strict faith'.

It would be sufficient, therefore, to put into words what is already more or less the practice, by proclaiming officially that adherence in one's heart to the mysteries of the Trinity, the Incarnation, Redemption, the Eucharist, and the revelatory character of the New Testament is the only condition of access to the sacraments.

In that case, without the danger of the Church exercising tyranny over people's souls, the Christian faith could be placed in the centre of secular life and of each of the activities which it comprises, and could impregnate everything, absolutely everything, with its light. This is the only hope of salvation for the wretched people of today.)

(*Pensées sans ordre*)

THREE ESSAYS ON
THE LOVE OF GOD

1. *Some thoughts on the Love of God*

To believe in God is not a decision that we can make. All we can do is to decide not to give our love to false gods. In the first place, we can decide not to believe that the future contains for us an all-sufficient good. The future is made of the same stuff as the present. We are well aware that the good which we possess at present, in the form of wealth, power, consideration, friends, the love of those we love, the well-being of those we love, and so on, is not sufficient; yet we believe that on the day when we get a little more we shall be satisfied. We believe this because we lie to ourselves. If we really reflect for a moment we know it is false. Or again, if we are suffering illness, poverty, or misfortune, we think we shall be satisfied on the day when it ceases. But there too, we know it is false; so soon as one has got used to not suffering one wants something else. In the second place, we can decide not to confuse the necessary with the good. There are a number of things which we believe to be necessary for our life. We are often wrong, because we should survive if we lost them. But even if we are right, even if they are things whose loss might kill us or at least destroy our vital energy, that does not make them good; because no one is satisfied for long with purely and simply living. One always wants something more; one wants something to live for. But it is only necessary to be honest with oneself to realize that there is nothing in this world to live for. We have only to imagine all our desires satisfied; after a time we should become discontented. We should want something else and we should be miserable through not knowing what to want.

A thing that everyone can do is to keep his attention fixed upon this truth.

Revolutionaries, for example, if they didn't lie to themselves, would know that the achievement of the revolution would make them unhappy, because they would lose their reason for living. And it is the same with all desires.

Life as it is given to men is unbearable without recourse to lying. Those who refuse to lie and who prefer to realize that life is unbearable, though without rebelling against fate, receive in the end, from somewhere beyond time, something which makes it possible to accept life as it is.

Everyone feels the existence of evil and feels horror at it and wants to get free from it. Evil is neither suffering nor sin; it is both at the same time, it is something common to them both. For they are linked together; sin makes us suffer and suffering makes us evil, and this indissoluble complex of suffering and sin is the evil in which we are submerged against our will, and to our horror.

A part of the evil that is within us we project into the objects of our attention and desire; and they reflect it back to us, as if the evil came from them. It is for this reason that any place where we find ourselves submerged in evil inspires us with hatred and disgust. It seems to us that the place itself is imprisoning us in evil. Thus an invalid comes to hate his room and the people around him, even if they are dear to him; and workers sometimes hate their factory, and so on.

But if through attention and love we project a part of our evil upon something perfectly pure, it cannot be defiled by it; it remains pure and does not reflect the evil back on us; and so we are delivered from the evil.

We are finite beings, and the evil in us is also finite; therefore by this method, if human life lasted long enough, we could be absolutely sure of being delivered in the end, in this world itself, from all evil.

The words of the Lord's Prayer are perfectly pure. Anyone who repeats the Lord's Prayer with no other intention than to bring to bear upon the words themselves the fullest attention of which he is capable is absolutely certain of being delivered in this way from a part, however small, of the evil he harbours within him. It is the same if one contemplates the Blessed Sacrament with no other thought except that Christ is there; and so on.

Nothing is pure in this world except sacred objects and

sacred texts, and the beauty of nature when looked at for itself and not as a background for day-dreams, and also, to a lesser degree, those human beings in whom God dwells and those works of art which are of divine inspiration.

That which is perfectly pure can be nothing other than God present in this world. If it were something other than God it would not be pure. If God were not present we could never be saved. In the soul in which this contact with purity has taken place, all its horror at the evil it harbours is changed into love for the divine purity. It was in this way that Mary Magdalene and the good thief became privileged by love.

The sole obstacle to the transmutation of horror into love is the self-regard which makes it painful to expose one's defilement to contact with purity. This can only be overcome if one has a kind of indifference about one's own defilement, so that one is capable of rejoicing, without regard to oneself, at the thought that something pure exists.

Contact with purity effects a transformation in evil. Only in this way can there be release from the indissoluble complex of suffering and sin. Through this contact, suffering gradually ceases to be mixed with sin; while sin transforms itself into simple suffering. This supernatural operation is called repentance. It is as though some joy were to shine upon the evil in us.

That there should have been one perfectly pure being present on earth was enough to make him the divine lamb which takes away the world's sin and to cause the greatest possible amount of the evil diffused around him to concentrate upon him in the form of suffering.

He has left some perfectly pure things as remembrances of himself; that is to say, things in which he is present, for otherwise their purity would fade away through being in contact with evil.

But people are not in churches all the time, and it is particularly desirable that this supernatural operation of transferring the evil from within oneself to outside should be able to occur in the places where everyday life is lived, and especially in places of work.

This can only be done through symbols making it possible

to read the divine truth in the circumstances of daily life and work in the same way that they are expressed in phrases by written letters. For this purpose the symbols must not be arbitrary but must be found inscribed, by a providential arrangement, in the very nature of things. The Gospel parables are an example of this symbolism.

There is indeed an analogy between the divine truths and the mechanical relations which constitute the order of the world of sense. The law of gravity which is sovereign on earth over all material motion is the image of the carnal attachment which governs the tendencies of the soul. The only power that can overcome gravity is solar energy. It is because this energy comes down to earth and is received by plants that they are able to grow vertically upwards. It enters into animals and men through the act of eating, and it is only thanks to this that we are able to hold ourselves erect and lift things up. Every source of mechanical energy – water power, coal, and very probably petroleum – derives in the same way from it; so it is the sun that drives our motors and lifts our aeroplanes, as it also lifts the birds. We cannot go and fetch this solar energy, we can only receive it. The energy comes down. It enters into plants and is with the seed, buried underground in darkness; it is there that its fertility becomes most active, inciting the movement from below upwards which makes the wheat or the tree grow. Even in a dead tree or a wooden beam it is still there, maintaining the vertical line; and we use it to build houses. It is the image of grace, which comes down to be buried in the darkness of our evil souls and is the only source of energy which can counteract the trend towards evil which is the moral law of gravity.

It is not the farmer's job to go in search of solar energy or even to make use of it, but to arrange everything in such a way that the plants capable of using it and transmitting it to us will receive it in the best possible conditions. And the effort he puts into this work does not come from himself but from the energy supplied to him by food, in other words, by this same solar energy contained in plants and in the flesh of animals nourished by plants. In the same way, the only effort we can make towards the good is so to dispose our soul that it can receive grace, and it is grace which supplies the energy needed for this effort.

A farmer or husbandman is like an actor continually playing a role in a sacred drama which represents the relations between God and the creation.

It is not only the source of solar energy that is inaccessible to man, but also the power which transforms this energy into food. Modern science considers this power to reside in the vegetable substance called chlorophyll; antiquity said sap instead of chlorophyll, but it comes to the same thing. Just as the sun is the image of God, so the vegetable sap – which can use the solar energy, and which makes plants and trees rise up straight in defiance of gravity, and which offers itself to be crushed and destroyed inside us and so to maintain our life – is the image of the Son, the Mediator. The farmer's whole work consists in serving this image.

Poetry like this should suffuse agricultural labour with a light of eternity. Without it, the work is so monotonous that the workers may easily sink into despairing apathy or seek the grossest relaxations; for their work reveals too obviously the futility which afflicts all human conditions. A man works himself to exhaustion in order to eat, and he eats in order to get strength to work, and after a year of labour everything is exactly as it was at the beginning. He works in a circle. Monotony is only bearable for man if it is lit up by the divine. But for this very reason a monotonous life is much the more propitious for salvation.

(*On Science, Necessity and the Love of God*, translated from *Pensées sans ordre*, Gallimard.)

2. *Some reflections on the Love of God*

The love that God bears us is, at any moment, the material
and substance of our very being. God's creative love which
maintains us in existence is not merely a superabundance of
generosity, it is also renunciation and sacrifice. Not only the
Passion but the Creation itself is a renunciation and sacrifice
on the part of God. The Passion is simply its consummation.
God already voids himself of his divinity by the Creation. He
takes the form of a slave, submits to necessity, abases himself.
His love maintains in existence, in a free and autonomous
existence, beings other than himself, beings other than the
good, mediocre beings. Through love, he abandons them to
affliction and sin. For if he did not abandon them they would
not exist. His presence would annul their existence as a flame
kills a butterfly.

Religion teaches that God created finite beings of different
degrees of mediocrity. We human beings are aware that we
are at the extreme limit, the limit beyond which it is no
longer possible to conceive or to love God. Below us there
are only the animals. We are as mediocre and as far from
God as it is possible for creatures endowed with reason to be.
This is a great privilege. It is for us, if he wants to come to
us, that God has to make the longest journey. When he has
possessed and won and transformed our hearts it is we in
our turn who have to make the longest journey in order to
go to him. The love is in proportion to the distance.

It was by an inconceivable love that God created beings
so distant from himself. It is by an inconceivable love that
he comes down so far as to reach them. It is by an inconceivable love that they then ascend so far as to reach him.
It is the same love. They can only ascend by the same love
which God bestowed on them when he came down to seek
them. And this is the same love by which he created them at
such a great distance from him. The Passion is not separable
from the Creation. The Creation itself is a kind of passion.
My very existence is like a laceration of God, a laceration
which is love. The more mediocre I am, the more obvious is
the immensity of the love which maintains me in existence.

The evil which we see everywhere in the world in the form of affliction and crime is a sign of the distance between us and God. But this distance is love and therefore it should be loved. This does not mean loving evil, but loving God through the evil. When a child in his play breaks something valuable, his mother does not love the breakage. But if later on her son goes far away or dies she thinks of the incident with infinite tenderness because she now sees it only as one of the signs of her child's existence. It is in this way that we ought to love God through everything good and everything evil, without distinction. If we love only through what is good, then it is not God we are loving but something earthly to which we give that name. We must not try to reduce evil to good by seeking compensations or justifications for evil. We must love God through the evil that occurs, solely because everything that actually occurs is real and behind all reality stands God. Some realities are more or less transparent; others are completely opaque; but God is behind all of them, without distinction. It is for us simply to keep our eyes turned towards the point where he is, whether we can see him or not. If there were no transparent realities we should have no idea of God. But if all realities were transparent it would not be God but simply the sensation of light that we would be loving. It is when we do not see God, it is when his reality is not sensibly perceptible to any part of our soul, that we have to become really detached from the self in order to love him. That is what it is to love God.

For this it is necessary to keep one's eyes constantly turned towards God, without ever moving. Otherwise, how should we know the right direction when the opaque screen comes between the light and us? We have to remain absolutely motionless.

To remain motionless does not mean to abstain from action. It is spiritual, not material immobility. But one must not act, or, indeed, abstain from acting, by one's own will. In the first place, we must perform only those acts to which we are constrained by a strict obligation, and then those which we honestly believe to have been enjoined upon us by God; and finally, if there remains an indefinite zone, those to which a natural inclination prompts us, provided they involve nothing illegitimate. In the sphere of action, it is only the fulfilment of strict obligations that calls for an effort. And, as for acts of obedience to God, they are performed passively; whatever pains may accompany them, they call for no effort, strictly speaking; it is not active effort but rather patience and capacity to endure and suffer. Their model is the crucifixion of Christ. Even though an act of obedience, when seen from outside, may seem accompanied by a great expenditure of activity there is in reality, within the soul, nothing but passive endurance.

There is, however, one effort to be made, and by far the hardest of all, but it is not in the sphere of action. It is keeping one's gaze directed towards God, bringing it back when it has wandered, and fixing it sometimes with all the intensity of which one is capable. This is very hard, because all the mediocre part of ourselves which is almost the whole of us – which *is* us, and is what we mean when we say 'I' – feels that this fixed gaze towards God condemns it to death. And it does not want to die. It rebels. It fabricates every falsehood that can possibly divert our attention.

One of these falsehoods is the false gods which are given the name of God. We may believe we are thinking about God when what we really love is certain people who have talked to us about him, or a certain social atmosphere, or certain ways of living, or a certain calm of soul, a certain source of joyful feeling, hope, comfort, or consolation. In such cases the mediocre part of the soul is perfectly safe; even prayer is no threat to it.

Another falsehood has to do with pleasure and pain. We are well aware that the lure of pleasure or the fear of pain sometimes makes us act, or fail to act, in ways which oblige us to turn our eyes away from God; and when this happens we think we have been conquered by pleasure or pain, but this is very often an illusion. Very often the pleasure or pain of the senses are simply a pretext employed by the mediocre part of us for turning away from God. In themselves they have not so much power; not even an intoxicating pleasure or a violent pain are so very difficult to renounce or endure. We see it done every day by very mediocre people. But

it is infinitely difficult to renounce even a very slight pleasure
or to expose oneself to a very slight pain solely for the sake
of God, the true God, that is to say, the one who is in
heaven and not anywhere else. Because to make that effort
is an approach, not towards suffering but towards death;
and towards a death which is more radical than that of the
body and equally repellent to nature: the death of the
thing within us that says 'I'.

It does sometimes happen that the flesh turns us away
from God, but often when we think this has happened it is
really the other way round. The soul being unable to bear
the deadly presence of God, that searing flame, takes refuge
behind the flesh and uses it like a screen. In this case it is not
the flesh which makes us forget God, it is the soul which
tries to forget God by burying itself within the flesh. This
is no longer a question of weakness but of treason, and we are
always tempted to this treason so long as the mediocre part
of the soul is much stronger than the part that is pure. A
fault very slight in itself may be an act of treason of this
kind, and in that case it is infinitely worse than faults which
are very bad in themselves but which are the result of weakness. Treason is not avoided by an effort, by doing violence
to oneself, but by a simple act of choice. It suffices to regard
as a stranger and enemy the part of us that wants to hide
itself from God – even if that part is almost the whole of us,
even if it *is* us. We must constantly renew within ourselves
the vow of adherence to that part of us which calls for
God, even when it is still only infinitely small. This infinitesimal part, so long as we adhere to it, increases exponentially
by a geometrical progression like the series 2, 4, 8, 16, 32,
etc., as a seed grows, and this happens without our taking
any part in the process. We can arrest this growth by
refusing it our adherence, and we can retard it by failing to
use our will against the unruly movements of the physical
part of the soul. But nevertheless when it does take place
this growth takes place in us without any action by us.

Another pitfall, another deception by the mediocre part of
us in its attempts to avoid death, is the misplaced effort towards the good, or towards God. This is a particularly dangerous deception because it is very difficult to understand why

such efforts are false. Everything seems to suggest that the mediocre part of us is much better informed than we are about the conditions of salvation, so that one is impelled to believe in the existence of something like the devil. There are people whose manner of seeking God is like a man making leaps into the air in the hope that, if he jumps a little higher each time, he will end by staying up there and rising into heaven. This is a vain hope. In Grimm's tale of 'The Valiant Little Tailor' there is a trial of strength between the little tailor and a giant. The giant hurls a stone high into the air, so that it takes a very, very long time to fall down again. The little tailor, who has a bird in his pocket, says he can do much better and that the stones he throws don't come down; and he releases his bird. Everything without wings always comes down to earth again. People who make athletic leaps towards heaven are too absorbed in the muscular effort to be able to look up to heaven; and in this matter the looking up is the one thing that counts. It is what makes God come down. And when God has come down to us he raises us, he gives us wings. The only effective and legitimate use of our muscular efforts is to keep at bay and suppress whatever may prevent us from looking up; they are negatively useful. The part of the soul which is capable of looking at God is surrounded by barking, biting, destructive dogs. They must be controlled by the whip. But there is also no objection to employing lumps of sugar when it is possible. In any case, whether by the whip or by sugar – both are in fact needed, in different proportions for different temperaments – what matters is to train the dogs and compel them to silence and immobility. This training is one of the conditions for spiritual ascension but it is not itself an elevating force. God alone is the elevating power, and he comes when we look towards him. To look towards him means to love him. There is no other relation between man and God except love. But our love for God should be like a woman's love for a man, which does not express itself by making advances but consists only in waiting. God is the Bridegroom, and it is for the bridegroom to come to the one he has chosen and speak to her and lead her away. The bride-to-be should only wait.

Pascal's words 'Thou wouldst not seek me if thou hadst not found me' are not the true expression of the relations between man and God. Plato is much more profound when he says 'Turn away with your whole soul from the things which pass.' It is not for man to seek, or even to believe in, God. He has only to refuse his love to everything which is not God. This refusal does not presuppose any belief. It is enough to recognize, what is obvious to any mind, that all the goods of this world, past, present or future, real or imaginary, are finite and limited and radically incapable of satisfying the desire which burns perpetually within us for an infinite and perfect good. All men know this, and more than once in their lives they recognize it for a moment, but then they immediately begin deceiving themselves again so as not to know it any longer, because they feel that if they knew it they could not go on living. And their feeling is true, for that knowledge kills, but it inflicts a death which leads to a resurrection. But they do not know that beforehand; all they foresee is death; they must either choose truth and death or falsehood and life. If one makes the first choice and holds to it, if one persists indefinitely in refusing to devote the whole of one's love to things unworthy of it, which means everything in this world without exception, that is enough. It is not a matter of self-questioning or searching. A man has only to persist in this refusal, and one day or another God will come to him. He will see and hear and cling to God, as Electra to Orestes; he will possess the certainty of an irrecusable reality. This does not mean that he will become incapable of doubting; to doubt is always both a faculty and a duty of the human mind; but doubt presents itself one has only to entertain it unreservedly of what is uncertain and confirms the certainty of what is certain. For any man of whom God has taken possession the doubt concerning the reality of God is purely abstract and verbal, much more abstract and verbal than the doubt concerning the reality of the things of sense. When such a doubt presents itself one has only to entertain it unreservedly to discover how abstract and verbal it is. Consequently, the problem of faith does not arise. Until God has taken possession of him, no human being can have faith, but only simple belief; and it hardly matters whether or not he has such a

belief because he will arrive at faith equally well through in-
credulity. The only choice before man is whether he will or
will not attach his love to this world. Let him refuse to
attach it, let him stay motionless, without searching, waiting
in immobility and without even trying to know what he
awaits, and it is absolutely certain that God will come all
the way to him. To search is to impede rather than to facili-
tate God's operation. The man of whom God has taken
possession no longer searches at all in the sense in which
Pascal seems to use the word search.

How could we search for God, since he is above, in a dimension not open to us? We can only advance horizontally; and
if we advance in this way, seeking our good, and the search
succeeds, this result will be illusory and what we have
found will not be God. A little child who suddenly perceives
that he has lost his mother in the street runs about, crying,
in all directions; but he is wrong. If he had the sense and
courage to stay where he is and wait, she would find him
sooner. We must only wait and call out. Not call upon
someone, while we still do not know if there *is* anyone; but
cry out that we are hungry and want bread. Whether we
cry for a long time or a short time, in the end we shall be
fed, and then we shall not believe but we shall *know* that there
really is bread. What surer proof could one ask for than
to have eaten it? But before one has eaten, it is neither
needful nor particularly useful to believe in bread. What is
essential is to know that one is hungry; and this is not
belief, it is absolutely certain knowledge which can only be
obscured by lies. All those who believe that food exists, or
will one day be produced, in this world, are lying.

The food of heaven not only makes the good grow in us but
it destroys the evil, which our own efforts can never do.
The quantity of evil in us can only be reduced by fixing our
gaze upon something perfectly pure.

(On *Science, Necessity and the Love of God*,
translated from *Pensées sans ordre*, Gallimard.)

3. *Additional pages on the Love of God and Affliction*

If the tree of life, and not simply the divine seed, is already formed in a man's soul at the time when extreme affliction strikes him, then he is nailed to the same cross as Christ.

Otherwise, there is the choice between the crosses on each side of Christ's.

We are like the impenitent thief if we seek consolation in contempt and hatred for our fellows in misfortune. This is the commonest effect of real affliction; it was so in the case of Roman slavery. People who are surprised when they observe such a state of mind in the afflicted would almost all fall into it themselves if affliction struck them.

To be like the good thief it is sufficient to remember that no matter what degree of affliction one is submerged in, one has deserved at least that much. Because it is certain that before being reduced to impotence by affliction one has been an accomplice, through cowardice, inertia, indifference, or culpable ignorance, in crimes which have plunged other human beings into an affliction at least as great. Generally, no doubt, we could not prevent those crimes, but we could express our reprobation of them. We neglected to do so, or even approved them, or at least we concurred in the expression of approval around us. For this complicity, the affliction we are suffering is not, in strict justice, too great a penalty. We have no right to feel compassion for ourselves. We know that at least once a perfectly innocent being suffered a worse affliction; it is better to direct our compassion to him across the centuries.

That is what everybody can and ought to say to himself. Because among our institutions and customs there are things so atrocious that nobody can legitimately feel himself innocent of this diffused complicity. It is certain that each of us is involved at least in the guilt of criminal indifference.

But in addition it is the right of every man to desire to have his part in Christ's own Cross. We have an unlimited right to ask God for everything that is good. In such demands there is no need for humility or moderation.

It is wrong to desire affliction; it is against nature, and it is a perversion; and moreover it is the essence of affliction that it is suffered unwillingly. So long as we are not submerged in affliction all we can do is to desire that, if it should come, it may be a participation in the Cross of Christ.

But what is in fact always present, and what it is therefore always permitted to love, is the possibility of affliction. All the three sides of our being are always exposed to it. Our flesh is fragile; it can be pierced or torn or crushed, or one of its internal mechanisms can be permanently deranged, by any piece of matter in motion. Our soul is vulnerable, being subject to fits of depression without cause and pitifully dependent upon all sorts of objects, inanimate and animate, which are themselves fragile and capricious. Our social personality, upon which our sense of existence almost depends, is always and entirely exposed to every hazard. These three parts of us are linked with the very centre of our being in such a way that it bleeds for any wound of the slightest consequence which they suffer. Above all, anything which diminishes or destroys our social prestige, our right to consideration, seems to impair or abolish our very essence – so much is our whole substance an affair of illusion.

When everything is going more or less well, we do not think about this almost infinite fragility. But nothing compels us not to think about it. We can contemplate it all the time and thank God for it unceasingly. We can be thankful not only for the fragility itself but also for that more intimate weakness which connects it with the very centre of our being. For it is this weakness which makes possible, in certain conditions, the operation by which we are nailed to the very centre of the Cross.

We can think of this fragility, with love and gratitude, on the occasion of any suffering, whether great or small. We can think of it at times when we are neither particularly happy nor unhappy. We can think of it whenever we experience any joy. This, however, we ought not to do if the thought were liable to cloud or lessen the joy. But it is not so. This thought only adds a more piercing sweetness to joy, in the same way that the flowers of the cherry are the more beautiful for being frail.

If we dispose our thought in this way, then after a certain

time the Cross of Christ should become the very substance
of our life. No doubt this is what Christ meant when he
advised his friends to bear their cross each day, and not,
as people seem to think nowadays, simply that one should be
resigned about one's little daily troubles – which, by an almost
sacrilegious abuse of language, people sometimes refer to as
crosses. There is only one cross; it is the whole of that
necessity by which the infinity of space and time is filled
and which, in given circumstances, can be concentrated upon
the atom that any one of us is, and totally pulverize it. To
bear one's cross is to bear the knowledge that one is entirely
subject to this blind necessity in every part of one's being,
except for one point in the soul which is so secret that it is
inaccessible to consciousness. However cruelly a man suffers,
if there is some part of his being still intact and if he is not
fully conscious that it has escaped only by chance and
remains every moment at the mercy of chance, he has no
part in the Cross. This is above all the case when the part of
the soul which remains intact, or even relatively intact, is the
social part; which is the reason why sickness profits nothing
unless there is added to it the spirit of poverty in its perfection. It is possible for a perfectly happy man – if he
recognizes, truly, concretely, and all the time, the possibility
of affliction – to enjoy happiness completely and at the same
time bear his cross.

But it is not enough to be aware of this possibility; one
must love it. One must tenderly love the harshness of that
necessity which is like a coin with two faces, the one turned
towards us being domination, and the one turned towards
God, obedience. We must embrace it closely even if it offers
its roughest surface and the roughness cuts into us. Any
lover is glad to clasp tightly some object belonging to an
absent loved one, even to the point where it cuts into the
flesh. We know that this universe is an object belonging to
God. We ought to thank God from the depth of our hearts
for giving us necessity, his mindless, sightless, and perfectly
obedient slave, as absolute sovereign. She drives us with a
whip. But being subject in this world to her tyranny, we
have only to choose God for our treasure, and put our heart
with it, and from that moment we shall see the other face

of the tyranny, the face which is pure obedience. We are the slaves of necessity, but we are also the sons of her Master. Whatever she demands of us, we ought to love the sight of her docility, we who are the children of the house. When she does not do as we wish, when she compels us to suffer what we would not, it is given us by means of love to pass through to the other side and to see the face of obedience which she turns towards God. Lucky are those to whom this precious opportunity comes often.

Intense and long-drawn-out physical pain has this unique advantage, that our sensibility is so made as to be unable to accept it. We can get used to, make the best of, and adapt ourselves to anything else except that; and we make the adaptation, in order to have the illusion of power, in order to believe that we are in control. We play at imagining that we have chosen what is forced upon us. But when a human being is transformed, in his own eyes, into a sort of animal, almost paralysed and altogether repulsive, he can no longer retain that illusion. It is all the better if this transformation is brought about by human wills, as a result of social re-probation, provided that it is not an honourable persecution but, as it were, a blind, anonymous oppression. In its physical part, the soul is aware of necessity only as constraint and is aware of constraint only as pain. It is the same truth which penetrates into the senses through pain, into the intelligence through mathematical proof, and into the faculty of love through beauty. So it was that to Job, when once the veil of flesh had been rent by affliction, the world's stark beauty was revealed. The beauty of the world appears when we recognize that the substance of the universe is necessity and that the substance of necessity is obedience to a perfectly wise Love. The universe of which we are a fraction has no other essence than to be obedient.

In the joy of the senses there is a virtue analogous to that of physical pain, if the joy is so vivid and pure, if it so far exceeds expectation, that we immediately recognize our inability to procure anything like it, or to retain its possession, by our own efforts. Of such joys, beauty is always the essence. Pure joy and pure pain are two aspects of the same infinitely precious truth. Fortunately so, because it is this that gives us the right to wish joy rather than pain to those we love.

The Trinity and the Cross are the two poles of Christianity, the two essential truths: the first, perfect joy; the second, perfect affliction. It is necessary to know both the one and the other and their mysterious unity, but the human condition in this world places us infinitely far from the Trinity, at the very foot of the Cross. Our country is the Cross.

The knowledge of affliction is the key of Christianity. But that knowledge is impossible. It is not possible to know affliction without having been through it. Thought is so revolted by affliction that it is as incapable of bringing itself voluntarily to conceive it as an animal, generally speaking, is incapable of suicide. Thought never knows affliction except by constraint. Unless constrained by experience, it is impossible to believe that everything in the soul – all its thoughts and feelings, its every attitude towards ideas, people, and the universe, and, above all, the most intimate attitude of the being towards itself – that all this is entirely at the mercy of circumstances. Even if one recognizes it theoretically, and it is rare indeed to do so, one does not believe it with all one's soul. To believe it with all one's soul is what Christ called, not renunciation or abnegation, as it is usually translated, but denying oneself; and it is by this that one deserves to be his disciple. But when we are in affliction or have passed through it we do not believe this truth any more than before; one could almost say that we believe it still less. Thought can never really be constrained; evasion by falsehood is always open to it. When thought finds itself, through the force of circumstance, brought face to face with affliction it takes immediate refuge in lies, like a hunted animal dashing for cover. Sometimes in its terror it burrows very deep into falsehood and it often happens that people who are or have been in affliction become addicted to lying as a vice, in some cases to such a degree that they lose the sense of any distinction between truth and falsehood in anything. It is wrong to blame them. Falsehood and affliction are so closely linked that Christ conquered the world simply because he, being the Truth, continued to be the Truth in the very depth of extreme affliction. Thought is constrained by an instinct of self-preservation to fly from the sight of affliction, and this instinct is infinitely more essential to our being than the instinct to avoid physical death. It is comparatively easy to face physical death so long as circumstances or the play of imagination present it under some other aspect than that of affliction. But to be able to face affliction with steady attention when it is close to him a man must be prepared, for the love of truth, to accept the death of the soul. This is the death of which Plato spoke when he said 'to philosophize is to learn to die'; it is the death which was symbolized in the initiation rites of the ancient mysteries, and which is represented by baptism. In reality, it is not a question of the soul's dying, but simply of recognizing the truth that it is a dead thing, something analogous to matter. It has no need to turn into water; it is water; the thing we believe to be our self is as ephemeral and automatic a product of external circumstances as the form of a sea-wave.

It is only necessary to know that, to know it in the depth of one's being. But to know humanity in that way belongs to God alone and to those in this world who have been re-generated from on high. For it is impossible to accept that death of the soul unless one possesses another life in addition to the soul's illusory life, unless one has placed one's treasure and one's heart elsewhere – and not merely outside one's person but outside all one's thoughts and feelings and outside everything knowable, in the hands of our Father who is in secret. Of those who have done this one can say that they have been born of water and the Spirit; for they are no longer anything except a two-fold obedience – on the one side to the mechanical necessity in which their earthly condition involves them, and on the other to the divine inspiration. There is nothing left in them which one could call their own will, their person, their 'I'. They have become nothing other than a certain intersection of nature and God. This intersection is the name with which God has named them from all eternity; it is their vocation. In the old baptism by immersion the man disappeared under the water; this means to deny one's self, to acknowledge that one is only a fragment of the inert matter which is the fabric of creation. He only reappeared because he was lifted up by an ascending movement stronger than gravity: this is the image of the divine love in man. Baptism contains the symbol of the state of perfection. The engagement it involves is the promise to desire that state and to beseech God for it, incessantly and untiringly, for as long as one has not obtained it – as a hungry child never stops asking his father for bread. But we cannot know what this promise commits us to until we encounter the terrible presence of affliction. It is only there, face to face with affliction, that the true commitment can be made, through a more secret, more mysterious, more miraculous contact even than a sacrament.

The knowledge of affliction being by nature impossible both to those who have experienced it and to those who have not, it is equally possible for both of them by supernatural favour; otherwise Christ would not have spared from affliction the man he cherished above all, and after having promised that he should drink from his cup. In both cases the knowledge of affliction is something much more miraculous than walking on water.

Those whom Christ recognized as his benefactors are those whose compassion rested upon the knowledge of affliction. The others give capriciously, irregularly, or else too regularly, or from habit imposed by training, or in conformity with social convention, or from vanity or emotional pity, or for the sake of a good conscience – in a word, from self-regarding motives. They are arrogant or patronizing or tactlessly sympathetic, or they let the afflicted man feel that they regard him simply as a specimen of a certain type of affliction. In any case, their gift is an injury. And they have their reward on earth, because their left hand is not unaware of what their right hand gave. Their contact with the afflicted must be a false one because the true understanding of the afflicted implies knowledge of affliction. Those who have not seen the face of affliction, or are not prepared to, can only approach the afflicted behind a veil of illusion or falsehood. If the look of affliction itself is revealed by chance on the face of the afflicted, they run away.

The benefactor of Christ, when he meets an afflicted man, does not feel any distance between himself and the other. He projects all his own being into him. It follows that the impulse

to give him food is as instinctive and immediate as it is for
oneself to eat when one is hungry. And it is forgotten almost
at once, just as one forgets yesterday's meals. Such a man
would not think of saying that he takes care of the afflicted
for the Lord's sake; it would seem as absurd to him as it
would be to say that he eats for the Lord's sake. One eats
because one can't help it. Christ will thank the people who
give in the way they eat.

They do for the afflicted something very different from
feeding, clothing, or taking care of them. By projecting their
own being into those they help they give them for a moment
– what affliction has deprived them of – an existence of their
own. Affliction is essentially a destruction of personality,
a lapse into anonymity. Just as Christ put off his divinity for
love, so the afflicted are stripped of their humanity by misfortune. In affliction, that misfortune itself becomes a man's
whole existence and in every other respect he loses all significance, in everybody's eyes including his own. There is
something in him that would like to exist, but it is continually pushed back into nothingness, like a drowning man
whose head is pushed under the water. He may be a pauper,
a refugee, a negro, an invalid, an ex-convict, or anything
of the kind; in any case, whether he is an object of ill usage
or of charity he will in either case be treated as a cipher,
as one item among many others in the statistics of a certain
type of affliction. So both good treatment and bad treatment
will have the same effect of compelling him to remain anonymous. They are two forms of the same offence.

The man who sees someone in affliction and projects into
him his own being brings to birth in him through love,
at least for a moment, an existence apart from his affliction.
For, although affliction is the occasion of this supernatural
process, it is not the cause. The cause is the identity of human
beings across all the apparent distances placed between them
by the hazards of fortune.

To project one's being into an afflicted person is to assume
for a moment his affliction, it is to choose voluntarily something whose very essence consists in being imposed by constraint upon the unwilling. And that is an impossibility. Only
Christ has done it. Only Christ and those men whose whole

soul he possesses can do it. What these men give to the afflicted whom they succour, when they project their own being into them, is not really their own being, because they no longer possess one; it is Christ himself.

Charity like this is a sacrament, a supernatural process by which a man in whom Christ dwells really puts Christ into the soul of the afflicted. If it is bread that is given, this bread is equivalent to the host. And this is not speaking symbolically or by conjecture, it is a literal translation of Christ's own words. He says: 'You have done it unto me.' Therefore he is in the naked or starving man. But he is not there in virtue of the nakedness or hunger, because affliction in itself contains no gift from above. Therefore Christ's presence can only be due to the operation of charity It is obvious that Christ is in the man whose charity is perfectly pure; for who could be Christ's benefactor except Christ himself? And it is easy to understand that only Christ's presence in a soul can put true compassion in it. But the Gospel reveals further that he who gives from true compassion gives Christ himself. The afflicted who receive this miraculous gift have the choice of consenting to it or not.

In affliction, if it is complete, a man is deprived of all human relationship. For him there are only two possible kinds of relation with men: the first, in which he figures only as a thing, is as mechanical as the relation between two contiguous drops of water, and the second is purely supernatural love. All relationships between these two extremes are forbidden him. There is no place in his life for anything except water and the Spirit. Affliction, when it is consented to and accepted and loved, is truly a baptism.

It is because Christ alone is capable of compassion that he received none while he was on earth. Being in the flesh in this world, he was not at the same time in the souls of those around him; and so there was no one to have pity on him. When suffering compelled him to seek pity, his closest friends refused it; they left him to suffer alone. Even John slept; and Peter, who had been able to walk on water, was incapable of pity when his master fell into affliction. So as to avoid seeing him, they took refuge in sleep. When Pity herself becomes affliction, where can she turn for help? It would have needed another Christ to have pity on Christ in affliction. In the centuries that followed, pity for Christ's affliction was one of the signs of sanctity.

The supernatural process of charity, as opposed to that of communion, for example, does not need to be completely conscious. Those whom Christ thanks reply: 'Lord, when . . .?' They did not know whom they were feeding. In general, there is nothing even to show that they knew anything at all about Christ. They may or they may not have. The important thing is that they were just; and because of that the Christ within them gave himself in the form of almsgiving. Beggars are fortunate people, in that there is a possibility of their receiving once or twice in their life such an alms.

Affliction is truly at the centre of Christianity. Through it is accomplished the sole and two-fold commandment: 'Love God', 'Love your neighbour.' For, as regards the first, it was said by Christ: 'No man cometh unto the Father, but by me'; and he also said: 'As Moses lifted up the serpent in the wilderness, even so must the Son of man be lifted up: that whosoever believeth in him should not perish, but have eternal life.' The serpent is that serpent of bronze which it was sufficient to look upon to be saved from the effects of poison. Therefore it is only by looking upon the Cross that we can love God. And as regards our neighbour, Christ has said who is the neighbour whom we are commanded to love. It is the naked, bleeding, and senseless body which we see lying in the road. What we are commanded to love first of all is affliction: the affliction of man, the affliction of God.

People often reproach Christianity for a morbid preoccupation with suffering and grief. This is an error. Christianity is not concerned with suffering and grief, for they are sensations, psychological states, in which a perverse indulgence is always possible; its concern is with something quite different, which is affliction. Affliction is not a psychological state; it is a pulverization of the soul by the mechanical brutality of circumstances. The transformation of a man, in his own eyes, from the human condition into that of a half-crushed worm writhing on the ground is a process which not even a pervert would find attractive. Neither does it attract a sage, a hero, or a saint. Affliction is something which imposes itself upon a man quite against his will. Its essence, the thing it is defined by, is the horror, the revulsion of the whole being, which it inspires in its victim. And this is the very thing one must consent to, by virtue of supernatural love.

It is our function in this world to consent to the existence of the universe. God is not satisfied with finding his creation good; he wants it also to find itself good. That is the purpose of the souls which are attached to minute fragments of this world; and it is the purpose of affliction to provide the occasion for judging that God's creation is good. Because, so long as the play of circumstance around us leaves our being almost intact, or only half impaired, we more or less believe that the world is created and controlled by ourselves. It is affliction that reveals, suddenly and to our very great surprise, that we are totally mistaken. After that, if we praise, it is really God's creation that we are praising. And where is the difficulty? We are well aware that divine glory is in no way diminished by our affliction; therefore we are in no way prevented from praising God for his great glory.

Thus, affliction is the surest sign that God wishes to be loved by us; it is the most precious evidence of his tenderness. It is something altogether different from a paternal chastisement, and could more justly be compared to the tender quarrels by which a young couple confirm the depth of their love. We dare not look affliction in the face; otherwise we should see after a little time that it is the face of love. In the same way Mary Magdalene perceived that he whom she took to be the gardener was someone else.

Seeing the central position occupied in their faith by affliction, Christians ought to suspect that it is in a sense the very essence of creation. To be a created thing is not necessarily to be afflicted, but it is necessarily to be exposed to affliction. Only the uncreated is indestructible. Those who ask why God permits affliction might as well ask why God created. And that, indeed, is a question one may well ask. Why did God create? It seems so obvious that God is greater than God and the creation together. At least, it seems obvious so long as one thinks of God as Being. But that is not how one ought to think of him. So soon as one thinks of God as Love one senses that marvel of love by which the Father and the Son are united both in the eternal unity of the one God and also across the separating distance of space and time and the Cross.

God is love, and nature is necessity; but this necessity, through obedience, is a mirror of love. In the same way, God is joy, and creation is affliction; but it is an affliction radiant with the light of joy. Affliction contains the truth about our condition. They alone will see God who prefer to recognize the truth and die, instead of living a long and happy existence in a state of illusion. One must want to go towards reality; then, when one thinks one has found a corpse, one meets an angel who says: 'He is risen.'

The Cross of Christ is the only source of light that is bright enough to illumine affliction. Wherever there is affliction, in any age or any country, the Cross of Christ is the truth of it. Any man, whatever his beliefs may be, has his part in the Cross of Christ if he loves truth to the point of facing affliction rather than escape into the depths of falsehood. If God had been willing to withhold Christ from the men of any given country or epoch, we should know it by an infallible sign: there would be no affliction among them. We know of no such period in history. Wherever there is affliction there is the Cross – concealed, but present to anyone who chooses truth rather than falsehood and love rather than hate. Affliction without the Cross is hell, and God has not placed hell upon the earth.

Conversely, there are many Christians who have no part in Christ because they lack the strength to recognize and worship the blessed Cross in every affliction. There is no such proof of feebleness of faith as the way in which people, even including Christians, sidetrack the problem of affliction when they discuss it. All the talk about original sin, God's will, Providence and its mysterious plans (which nevertheless one thinks one can try to fathom), and future recompenses of every kind in this world and the next, all this only serves to conceal the reality of affliction, or else fails to meet the case. There is only one thing that enables us to accept real affliction, and that is the contemplation of Christ's Cross. There is nothing else. That one thing suffices.

A mother, a wife, or a fiancée, if they know that the

person they love is in distress, will want to help him and be with him, and if that is impossible they will at least seek to lessen their distance from him and lighten the heavy burden of impotent sympathy by suffering some equivalent distress. Whoever loves Christ and thinks of him on the Cross should feel a similar relief when gripped by affliction.

By reason of the essential link between the Cross and affliction, no State has the right to dissociate itself from all religion except on the absurd hypothesis that it has succeeded in abolishing affliction. *A fortiori* it has no such right if it is itself creating affliction. A penal system entirely dissociated from any reference to God has a really infernal aura. Not on account of wrong verdicts or excessive punishments but, apart from all that, in itself. It defiles itself by contact with every defilement, and since it contains no purifying principle it becomes so polluted that it can further degrade even the most degraded criminal. Contact with it is hideous for anyone with any integrity or health of mind; and, as for the corrupt, they find an even more horribly corrupt sort of appeasement in the very punishments it inflicts. Nothing is pure enough to bring purity to the places reserved for crime and punishment except Christ, who was himself condemned by the law.

But it is only the Cross, and not the complications of dogma, that is needed by States; and it is disastrous that the Cross and dogma have become so closely linked. By this link, Christ has been drawn away from the criminals who are his brothers.

The idea of necessity as the material common to art, science, and every kind of labour is the door by which Christianity can enter profane life and permeate the whole of it. For the Cross is necessity itself brought into contact with the lowest and the highest part of us; with our physical sensibility by its evocation of physical pain and with supernatural love by the presence of God. It thus involves the whole range of contacts with necessity which are possible for the intermediate parts of our being.

There is not, there cannot be, any human activity in whatever sphere, of which Christ's Cross is not the supreme and secret truth. No activity can be separated from it without rotting or shrivelling like a cut vine-shoot. That is what is happening today, before our uncomprehending eyes, while we ask ourselves what has gone wrong. And Christians comprehend least of all because, knowing that the roots of our activities go back long before Christ, they cannot understand that the Christian faith is the sap in them.

But this would be no problem if we understood that the Christian faith, under veils which do not obscure its radiance, comes to flower and fruit at every time and every place where there are men who do not hate the light.

Never since the dawn of history, except for a certain period of the Roman Empire, has Christ been so absent as today. The separation of religion from the rest of social life, which seems natural even to the majority of Christians nowadays, would have been judged monstrous by antiquity.

The sap of Christianity should be made to flow everywhere in the life of society; but nevertheless it is destined above all for man in solitude. The Father is in secret, and there is no secret more inviolable than affliction.

There is a question which is absolutely meaningless and therefore, of course, unanswerable, and which we normally never ask ourselves, but in affliction the soul is constrained to repeat it incessantly like a sustained, monotonous groan. This question is: Why? Why are things as they are? The afflicted man naïvely seeks an answer, from men, from things, from God, even if he disbelieves in him, from anything or everything. Why is it necessary precisely that he should have nothing to eat, or be worn out with fatigue and brutal treatment, or be about to be executed, or be ill, or be in prison? If one explained to him the causes which have produced his present situation, and this is in any case seldom possible because of the complex interaction of circumstances, it will not seem to him to be an answer. For his question 'Why?' does not mean 'By what cause?' but 'For what purpose?' And it is impossible, of course, to indicate any purposes to him; unless we invent some imaginary ones, but that sort of invention is not a good thing.

It is singular that the affliction of other people, except sometimes though not always, those very close to us, does not provoke this question. At the most, it may occur to us casually for a moment. But so soon as a man falls into affliction the question takes hold and goes on repeating itself incessantly. Why? Why? Why? Christ himself asked it: 'Why hast thou forsaken me?'

There can be no answer to the 'Why?' of the afflicted, because the world is necessity and not purpose. If there were finality in the world, the place of the good would not be in the other world. Whenever we look for final causes in this world it refuses them. But to know that it refuses, one has to ask.

The only things that compel us to ask the question are affliction, and also beauty; for the beautiful gives us such a vivid sense of the presence of something good that we look for some purpose there, without even finding one. Like affliction, beauty compels us to ask: Why? Why is this thing beautiful? But rare are those who are capable of asking themselves this question for as long as a few hours at a time. The afflicted man's question goes on for hours, days, years; it ceases only when he has no strength left.

He who is capable not only of crying out but also of listening will hear the answer. Silence is the answer. This is the eternal silence for which Vigny bitterly reproached God; but Vigny had no right to say how the just man should reply to the silence, for he was not one of the just. The just man loves. He who is capable not only of listening but also of loving hears this silence as the word of God.

The speech of created beings is with sounds. The word of God is silence. God's secret word of love can be nothing else but silence. Christ is the silence of God.

Just as there is no tree like the Cross, so there is no harmony like the silence of God. The Pythagoreans discerned this harmony in the fathomless eternal silence around the stars. In this world, necessity is the vibration of God's silence.

Our soul is constantly clamorous with noise, but there is one point in it which is silence, and which we never hear. When the silence of God comes to the soul and penetrates it and joins the silence which is secretly present in us, from then on we have our treasure and our heart in God; and space opens before us as the opening fruit of a plant divides in two, for we are seeing the universe from a point situated outside space.

This operation can take place in only two ways, to the exclusion of all others. There are only two things piercing enough to penetrate our souls in this way; they are affliction and beauty.

Often, one could weep tears of blood to think how many unfortunates are crushed by affliction without knowing how to make use of it. But, coolly considered, this is not a more pitiful waste than the squandering of the world's beauty. The brightness of stars, the sound of sea-waves, the silence of the hour before dawn – how often do they not offer themselves in vain to men's attention? To pay no attention to the world's beauty is, perhaps, so great a crime of ingratitude that it deserves the punishment of affliction. To be sure, it does not always get it; but then the alternative punishment is a mediocre life, and in what way is a mediocre life preferable to affliction? Moreover, even in the case of great misfortune such people's lives are probably still mediocre. So far as conjecture is possible about sensibility, it would seem that the evil within a man is a protection against the external evil that attacks him in the form of pain. One must hope it is so, and that for the impenitent thief God has mercifully reduced to insignificance such useless suffering. In fact, it certainly is so, because that is the great temptation which affliction offers; it is always possible for an afflicted man to suffer less by consenting to become wicked.

The man who has known pure joy, if only for a moment, and who has therefore tasted the flavour of the world's beauty, for it is the same thing, is the only man for whom affliction is something devastating. At the same time, he is the only man who has not deserved this punishment. But, after all, for him it is no punishment; it is God himself holding his hand and pressing it rather hard. For, if he remains constant, what he will discover buried deep under the sound of his own lamentations is the pearl of the silence of God.

(On *Science, Necessity and the Love of God*, translated from *Pensées sans ordre*, Gallimard.)

LETTER
TO A PRIEST

When I read the catechism of the Council of Trent, it seems as though I had nothing in common with the religion there set forth. When I read the New Testament, the mystics, the liturgy, when I watch the celebration of the mass, I feel with a sort of conviction that this faith is mine or, to be more precise, would be mine without the distance placed between it and me by my imperfection. This results in a painful spiritual state. I would like to make it, not less painful, only clearer. Any pain whatsoever, is acceptable where there is clarity.

I am going to enumerate for you a certain number of thoughts which have dwelt in me for years (some of them at least) and which form a barrier between me and the Church. I do not ask you to discuss their basis. I should be happy for there to be such a discussion, but later on, in the second place.

I ask you to give me a definite answer – leaving out such expressions as 'I think that', etc. – regarding the compatibility or incompatibility of each of these opinions with membership of the Church. If there is any incompatibility, I should like you to say straight out: I would refuse baptism (or absolution) to anybody claiming to hold the opinions expressed under the headings numbered so-and-so, so-and-so and so-and-so. I do not ask for a quick answer. There is no hurry. All I ask for is a categorical answer.

I must apologize for giving you this trouble, but I do not see how I can avoid it. I am far from regarding meditation on these problems as a game. Not only is it of more than vital importance, seeing that one's eternal salvation is at stake; but, furthermore, it is of an importance which far surpasses in my opinion that of my own salvation. A problem of life and death is a game by comparison.

Among the opinions that are to follow there are some about which I am doubtful; but were it a strict article of the faith to esteem them false, I should regard them as being as serious an obstacle as the others, for I am firmly convinced that they are held in doubt by me, that is to say, that it is not legitimate to deny them categorically.

Some of these opinions (more particularly those which concern the Mysteries, the Scriptures not of Jewish-Christian inspiration, Melchisedec, etc.) have never been condemned, although it is very likely that they were upheld in the early centuries. This makes me wonder if they were not secretly accepted. However that may be, if today they were to be publicly proclaimed by me or by others and condemned by the Church, I would not abandon them, unless it could be proved to me that they were false.

I have been thinking about these things for years with all the intensity of love and attention of which I am capable. This intensity is a wretchedly feeble one because of my imperfection which is very great; but it seems to me it is always on the increase. In proportion as it grows, the bonds which attach me to the Catholic faith become ever stronger and stronger, ever more deeply rooted in the heart and intelligence. But at the same time the thoughts which separate me from the Church also gain in force and clarity. If these thoughts are really incompatible with membership of the Church, then there is no hope that I may ever take part in the sacraments. If such is the case, I do not see how I can avoid the conclusion that my vocation is to be a Christian outside the Church. The possibility of there being such a vocation would imply that the Church is not Catholic in fact as it is in name, and that it must one day become so, if it is destined to fulfil its mission.

The opinions which follow have for me various degrees of probability or certainty, but all go accompanied in my mind by a question-mark. If I express them in the indicative mood it is only because of the poverty of language; my needs would require that the conjugation should contain a supplementary tense. In the domain of holy things I affirm nothing categorically. But such of my opinions as are in conformity with the teaching of the Church also go accompanied in my mind by the same question-mark.

I look upon a certain suspension of judgment with regard to all thoughts whatever they may be, without any exception, as constituting the virtue of humility in the domain of the intelligence.

Here is the list:

I

If we take a moment in history anterior to Christ and sufficiently remote from him – for example, five centuries before his time – and we set aside what follows afterwards, at that moment Israel has less of a share in God and in divine truth than several of the surrounding peoples (India, Egypt, Greece, China). For the essential truth concerning God is that he is good. To believe that God can order men to commit atrocious acts of injustice and cruelty is the greatest mistake it is possible to make with regard to him.

Zeus, in the *Iliad*, orders no cruelty whatever. The Greeks believed that 'suppliant Zeus' inhabits every miserable creature that implores pity. Jehovah is the 'God of hosts'. The history of the Hebrews shows that this refers not only to the stars, but also to the warriors of Israel. Now, Herodotus enumerates a great number of Hellenic and Asiatic peoples amongst whom there was *only one* that had a 'Zeus of hosts'. This blasphemy was unknown to all the others. The Egyptian *Book of the Dead*, at least three thousand years old, and doubtless very much older, is filled with evangelic charity. (The dead man says to Osiris: 'Lord of Truth, I bring thee the truth . . . I have destroyed evil for thee . . . I have killed no man. I have made no man weep. I have let no man suffer hunger. I have never been the cause of a master's doing harm to his slave. I have never made any man afraid. I have never adopted a haughty tone. I have never turned a deaf ear to just and true words. I have never put my name forward for honours. I have not spurned God in his manifestations. . . .')

The Hebrews, who for four centuries were in contact with Egyptian civilization, refused to adopt this sweet spirit. They wanted power. . . .

All the texts dating from before the exile are, I think, tainted with this fundamental error concerning God – except the Book of Job, the hero of which is not a Jew, the Song of Solomon (but does it date from before the exile?) and certain psalms of David (but have they been correctly attributed?). Otherwise, the first absolutely pure character appearing in Jewish history is Daniel (who was initiated into Chaldean lore). The lives of all the others, beginning with Abraham, are sullied by atrocious things. (Abraham starts off by prostituting his wife.)

This would incline one to think that Israel learnt the most essential truth about God (namely, that God is good before being powerful) from foreign traditional sources, Chaldean, Persian or Greek, and thanks to the exile.

2

What we call idolatry is to a large extent an invention of Jewish fanaticism. All peoples at all times have always been monotheistic. If some Hebrews of classical Jewry were to return to life and were to be provided with arms, they would exterminate the lot of us – men, women and children, for the crime of idolatry. They would reproach us for worshipping Baal and Astarte, taking Christ for Baal and the Virgin for Astarte.

Conversely, Baal and Astarte were perhaps representations of Christ and the Virgin.

Some of these cults have been justly accused of the debauches that accompanied them – but, I think, far less often than it is supposed today.

But the cruelties bound up with the cult of Jehovah, the exterminations commanded by him, are defilements at least as atrocious. Cruelty is a still more appalling crime than lust. Moreover, lust satisfies itself as readily by murder as it does by sexual intercourse.

The feelings of the so-called pagans for their statues were very probably the same as those inspired nowadays by the crucifix and the statues of the Virgin, with the same deviations among people of mediocre spiritual and intellectual development.

Is not such-and-such a supernatural virtue commonly attributed to some particular statue of the Virgin?

Even if they did happen to believe the divinity to be totally present in some stone or wood, it may be they were sometimes right. Do we not believe God is present in some bread and wine? Perhaps God was actually present in statues fashioned and consecrated according to certain rites.

The veritable idolatry is covetousness (*pleonexia hétis estiv idolatreia* Colossians 3:5), and the Jewish nation, in its thirst for carnal good, was guilty of this in the very moments even when it was worshipping its God. The Hebrews took for their idol, not something made of metal or wood, but a race, a nation, something just as earthly. Their religion is essentially inseparable from such idolatry, because of the notion of the 'chosen people'.

3

The ceremonies of the Eleusinian mysteries and of those of Osiris were regarded as sacraments in the sense in which we understand that term today. And *it may be* they were real sacraments, possessing the same virtue as baptism or the eucharist, and deriving that virtue from the same relation with Christ's Passion. The Passion was then to come. Today it is past. Past and future are symmetrical. Chronology cannot play a decisive role in a relationship between God and man, a relationship one of the terms of which is eternal.

If the Redemption, with the sensible signs and means corresponding to it, had not been present on this earth from the very beginning, it would not be possible to pardon God – if one may use such words without blasphemy – for the affliction of so many innocent people, so many people uprooted, enslaved, tortured and put to death in the course of centuries preceding the Christian era. Christ is present on this earth, unless men drive him away, wherever there is crime and affliction. Without the supernatural effects of this presence, how would the innocent, crushed beneath the weight of affliction, be able to avoid falling into the crime of cursing God, and consequently into damnation?

Moreover, St John talks about the 'Lamb slain from the

foundation of the world'.

The proof that the content of Christianity existed before Christ is that since his day there have been no very noticeable changes in men's behaviour.

4

There have *perhaps* been among various people (India, Egypt, China, Greece) sacred Scriptures revealed in the same manner as the Jewish-Christian Scriptures. Some of the texts which still exist today are possibly either fragments or echoes of them.

5

The passages in the Bible (Genesis, Psalms, St Paul) concerning Melchisedec prove that from the dawn of Israel there existed outside Israel a service of and knowledge of God situated on the selfsame level as Christianity and infinitely superior to anything Israel itself has ever possessed.

There is nothing to exclude the supposition of a link between Melchisedec and the ancient mysteries. There is an affinity between bread and Demeter, wine and Dionysus.

Melchisedec is apparently, according to Genesis, a king of Canaan. Hence, in all probability, the corruption and impiety of the villages of Canaan either dated back only a few centuries at the time of the massacres, or else were libellous inventions levelled against their victims by the Hebrews.

6

The passage in St Paul concerning Melchisedec, taken in connection with Christ's words 'Abraham hath seen my day', might even indicate that Melchisedec was already an Incarnation of the Word.

At all events, we do not know for certain that there have not been incarnations previous to that of Jesus, and that Osiris in Egypt, Krishna in India were not of that number.

7

If Osiris is not a man having lived on earth while remaining God, in the same way as Christ, then at any rate the story of Osiris is a prophecy infinitely clearer, more complete and closer to the truth than everything which goes by that name in the Old Testament. The same applies to other gods that have died and returned to life.

The extreme importance *at the present day* of this problem comes from the fact that it is becoming a matter of urgency to remedy the divorce which has existed for twenty centuries and goes on getting worse and worse between profane civilization and spirituality in Christian countries. Our civilization owes nothing to Israel and very little to Christianity; it owes nearly everything to pre-Christian antiquity (Germans, Druids, Rome, Greece, Aegeo-Cretans, Phoenicians, Egyptians, Babylonians . . .). If there is a watertight division between this antiquity and Christianity, the same watertight division exists between our profane life and our spiritual life. For Christianity to become truly incarnated, for the whole of life to become permeated by the Christian inspiration, it must first of all be recognized that, historically, our profane civilization is derived from a religious inspiration which, although chronologically pre-Christian, was Christian in essence. God's wisdom must be regarded as the unique source of all light upon earth, even such feeble lights as those which illumine the things of this world.

And the same applies in the case of Prometheus. The story of Prometheus is the very story of Christ projected into the eternal. All that is wanting is its localization in time and space.

Greek mythology is full of prophecies; so are the stories drawn from European folklore, what are known as fairy tales.

Many of the names of Greek divinities are probably in reality various names for designating one single divine Person, namely the Word. I think this is so in the case of Dionysus, Apollo, Artemis, celestial Aphrodite, Prometheus, Eros, Proserpina and several others.

I also think that Hestia, Athene and possibly Hephaestus are names for the Holy Spirit. Hestia is the central Fire. Athene came forth from the head of Zeus after the latter had devoured his wife, Wisdom, who was pregnant; she 'proceeds', therefore, from God and his Wisdom. Her emblem is the olive, and oil, in the Christian sacraments, is symbolically connected with the Holy Spirit.

Certain actions performed by Christ, certain words of his are constantly commented upon as follows: 'The prophecies must needs be fulfilled.' This refers to the Hebrew prophecies. But there are other actions, other words which might be commented upon in the same way in connection with the non-Hebrew prophecies.

Christ began his public life by changing the water into wine. He ended it by transforming the wine into blood. He thus marked his affinity to Dionysus. And again by the words: 'I am the true vine.'

The words: 'Except a corn of wheat die' express his affinity to the dead and resuscitated divinities which were represented by vegetation, such as Attis and Proserpina.

The motherhood of the Virgin has mysterious connections with some words in Plato's *Timaeus* concerning a certain essence, mother of all things and for ever intact. All the mother Goddesses of antiquity, like Demeter, Isis, were figures of the Virgin.

The comparison again and again insisted upon between the Cross and a tree, between the crucifixion and a hanging, must be connected with mythologies that have now disappeared.

If the date of the Scandinavian poem the *Rune of Odin* is prior to any possible Christian influence (which is unverifiable), it also contains a very striking prophecy:

'I know that I hung on a wind-swept tree for nine full nights, pierced with a spear and offered up to Odin, I to myself; on the tree whereof no man can tell what are the roots from which it springs.

'None gave me bread, or a horn to drink from. I looked down, I applied myself to the runes, weeping I learnt them, then I came down from there.' (First Edda.)

The term 'Lamb of God' is no doubt connected with traditions having possibly links with what is nowadays called

totemism. The story of Zeus Ammon in Herodotus (Zeus slay-
ing a ram in order to appear, covered with its fleece, before
the person who entreats him to allow himself to be seen),
considered in connection with the words of St John: 'The
Lamb slain from the foundation of the world', throws a pene-
trating light on this subject. The first sacrifice that was pleasing
to God, that of Abel, recalled in the canon of the mass as
an image of that of Christ, was an animal sacrifice. The same
applies in the case of the second one, Noah's, which defin-
itively saved humanity from the wrath of God and brought
about a pact between God and mankind. These are precisely
the effects of Christ's Passion. There is a very mysterious
relationship between the two.

People must have thought in very ancient times that God
is actually present in animals killed to be eaten; that God
in fact descends into them for the purpose of offering himself as food to man. This notion turned animal food into a
communion, whereas otherwise it is a crime, unless we adopt
a more or less Cartesian philosophy.[1]

Perhaps at Thebes, in Egypt, God was actually present in
the ram sacrificed ritually, as he is today in the consecrated
host.

It is worth noticing that at the moment Christ was crucified, the sun was in the constellation of the Ram.

Plato, in *Timaeus*, describes the astronomical constitution of
the universe as a sort of crucifixion of the Soul of the World,
the point of intersection being the equinoctial point, that is to
say, the constellation of the Ram.

Several texts (*Epinomis, Timaeus, Symposium*, Philolaos,
Proclus) indicate that the geometrical construction of the
proportional mean between a number and unity – the central
fact in Greek geometry – was the symbol of the divine
mediation between God and man.

Now, a considerable number of Christ's sayings reported
in the Gospels (especially St John) have with a very marked
insistence, which can only have been designed intentionally, the
algebraical form of the proportional mean. For example: 'As
my Father hath sent me, even so send I you, etc.' A single
relationship unites the Father to Christ, Christ to his disciples.

[1] Old Testament.

Christ is the proportional mean between God and the Saints.
The very word mediation indicates this.

From this I conclude that just as Christ recognized himself
in the Messiah of the Psalms, the Just One who suffers in
Isaiah, the bronze serpent of Genesis, so in the same way he
recognized himself in the proportional mean of Greek geometry, which thus becomes the most resplendent of the prophecies.

Ennius, in a Pythagorean writing, says: 'The moon is
called Proserpina . . . because, *like a serpent*, she is twisted
now towards the left now towards the right.'

All the mediatory gods that may be likened to the Word
are lunar gods, wearers of horns, lyres or bows representing the
crescent moon (Osiris, Artemis, Apollo, Hermes, Dionysus,
Zagreus, Eros . . .). Prometheus forms an exception, but in
Aeschylus Io stands for his counterpart, condemned to per-
petual vagabondage as he is to crucifixion – and she is horned.
(It is worth remembering that before he was crucified Christ
was a vagabond – and Plato depicts Eros as a wretched vagabond.)

If the Sun is the image of the Father, the Moon, perfect
reflection of solar splendour, but a reflection we can gaze
upon and which suffers diminution and disappearance, is the
image of the Son. The light is then that of the Spirit.

Heraclitus recognized a Trinity, which we can only divine
from the fragments of his that remain to us, but which stands
out clearly in the *Hymn to Zeus* of Cleanthus of Heraclitian
inspiration. The Persons are: Zeus, the Logos and the divine
Fire or Lightning.

Cleanthus says to Zeus: 'This universe *consents* to thy
domination (*hekon krateitai*) – Such is the virtue of the servitor that thou holdest under thine invincible hands – Flaming,
two-edged, eternally living, the lightning.' The lightning is not
an instrument of coercion, but a fire which arouses voluntary
consent and obedience. It is therefore Love. And this Love is
a servitor, an eternally living presence, hence a Person. Those
very ancient representations of Zeus with a two-edged axe
(symbol of lightning) on Cretan bas-reliefs already possessed
perhaps this significance. We may draw the parallel between
'two-edged' and Christ's words: 'I am not come to bring
peace, but a sword.'

Fire is constantly the symbol of the Holy Spirit in the New Testament.

The Stoics, heirs of Heraclitus, named *pneuma* the fire whose energy sustains the order of the world. *Pneuma*, that is fiery breath.

The semen which produces carnal generation was, according to them and according to the Pythagoreans, a *pneuma* mixed with liquid.

Christ's words about being born anew – and consequently the whole symbolism of baptism – must so as to be properly understood be considered more particularly in relation to the Pythagorean and Stoic conceptions concerning generation. Justin, moreover, I think, compares baptism to generation. Hence the Orphic words : 'Kid, thou art fallen into milk' must perhaps be understood in connection with baptism (the Ancients looked upon milk as being composed of the father's seminal fluid).

The celebrated expression 'Great Pan is dead' was perhaps meant to announce, not the disappearance of idolatry, but the death of Christ – Christ being the Great Pan, the great All. Plato (*Cratylus*) says that Pan is the 'logos'. In *Timaeus* he gives this name to the Soul of the World.

St John, in making use of the words Logos and Pneuma, indicated the profound relationship existing between Greek Stoicism (to be distinguished from that of Cato and Brutus!) and Christianity.

Plato also clearly recognized and by allusions in his works pointed to the dogmas of the Trinity, Mediation, the Incarnation, the Passion, and to the notions of grace and salvation through love. He recognized the essential truth, namely, that God is the Good. He is only the All-powerful by way of addition.

In saying : 'I am come to send fire on the earth; and what will I, if it be already kindled?', Christ indicated his kinship with Prometheus.

His words : 'I am the Way' should be compared with the Chinese 'Tao', a word signifying literally 'the way' and metaphorically, on the one hand the method of salvation, and on the other hand the impersonal God who is the God of Chinese spirituality, but who, although impersonal, is the model for the wise and acts continually.

His words: 'I am the Truth' call to mind Osiris, Lord of Truth.

When in one of his most important teachings he says: 'They which do the truth' (*poiountes alétheian*), he uses an expression which is not a Greek one, and which, as far as I know, is not a Hebrew one (must verify this). On the other hand, it is an Egyptian one. *Maât* means at the same time justice and truth. That is significant. No doubt it is not for nothing that the Holy Family went down into Egypt.

Baptism regarded as a death is the equivalent of the ancient initiations. St Clement of Rome uses the word 'initiated' in the sense of baptized. The use of the word 'mysteries' to designate the sacraments points to the same equivalence. The circular font strongly resembles the stone basin in which, according to Herodotus, the mystery of Osiris's passion was celebrated. They both represent perhaps the open sea, that open sea on which floated Noah's ark and that of Osiris, wooden structures which saved humanity before the one of the Cross.

Any number of accounts drawn from mythology and folk-lore could be translated into Christian truths without forcing or deforming anything in them, but rather, on the contrary, thus throwing a vivid light upon them. And these truths would, in their turn, thereby take on a new clarity.

8

Every time that a man has, with a pure heart called upon Osiris, Dionysus, Krishna, Buddha, the Tao, etc., the Son of God has answered him by sending the Holy Spirit. And the Holy Spirit has acted upon his soul, not by inciting him to abandon his religious tradition, but by bestowing upon him light – and in the best of cases the fulness of light – in the heart of that same religious tradition.

Prayer with the Greeks bore a strong resemblance to Christian prayer. When Aeschylus says, in the *Frogs* of Aristophanes: "Demeter, thou who hast nourished my thoughts, may I be worthy of thy mysteries!', that strongly resembles a prayer to the Virgin, and must have had the same virtue. Aeschylus gives a perfect description of contemplation in the magnificent lines: 'Whosoever, his thoughts turned toward Zeus, shall proclaim his glory, the same shall receive the fulness of wisdom.' (He recognized the Trinity: '. . . by the side of Zeus there stand his act and his word'.)

It is, therefore, useless to send out missions to prevail upon the peoples of Asia, Africa or Oceania to enter the Church.

9

When Christ said: 'Go ye therefore, and teach all nations, and bring them the glad tidings,' he commanded his apostles to bring glad tidings, not a theology. He himself, having come, as he said, 'only for the sheep of the house of Israel', added these good tidings on to the religion of Israel.

He probably wished that each of the apostles should in the same way add the good tidings of the life and death of Christ on to the religion of the country in which he happened to find himself. But the command was misunderstood, because of the ineradicable nationalism of the Jews. They must needs impose their Scriptures everywhere.

If it is thought that it shows a lot of presumption to suppose that the apostles misunderstood Christ's commands, I can only answer that there is no doubt at all that they did display incomprehension with regard to certain points. For after Christ had risen and had said: Go and teach the nations (or the Gentiles) and baptize them; after he had spent forty days with his disciples revealing his doctrine to them, Peter had to have, nevertheless, a special revelation and a dream before being able to make up his mind to baptize a heathen; he found it necessary to invoke this dream in order to explain this action to his followers; and Paul had great difficulty in eliminating circumcision.

Besides, it is written that the tree shall be known by its fruits. The Church has borne too many evil fruits for there not to have been some mistake made at the beginning.

Europe has been spiritually uprooted, cut off from that antiquity in which all the elements of our civilization have their origin; and she has gone about uprooting the other continents from the sixteenth century onwards.

After twenty centuries, Christianity has, practically speaking, not penetrated outside the white race; Catholicism is much more limited still in extent. America remained for sixteen centuries without hearing Christ spoken of (yet St Paul had said: Glad Tidings which have been announced to the *whole* of creation) and the nations living there were destroyed in the midst of the most appalling cruelties before ever having had the time to know him. Missionary zeal has not Christianized Africa, Asia and Oceania, but has brought these territories under the cold, cruel and destructive dominion of the white race, which has trodden down everything.

It would be strange, indeed, that the word of Christ should have produced such results if it had been properly understood.

Christ said: 'Go ye, and teach all nations and baptize those who believe', that is to say, those who believe in him. He never said: 'Compel them to renounce all that their ancestors have looked upon as sacred, and to adopt as a holy book the history of a small nation unknown to them.' I have been assured that the Hindus would in no way be prevented by their own tradition from receiving baptism, were it not for the fact that the missionaries make it a condition that they must renounce Vishnu and Shiva. If a Hindu believes that Vishnu is the Word and Shiva the Holy Spirit, and that the Word was incarnate in Krishna and in Rama before being so in Jesus, by what right can he be refused baptism? In the same way, in the quarrel between the Jesuits and the Papacy over the missions in China, it was the Jesuits who were carrying out the words of Christ.

10

Missionary action in the way in which it is, in fact, conducted (especially since the condemnation of Jesuit policy in China in the seventeenth century) is bad, save perhaps in certain individual cases. The missionaries – even the martyrs amongst them – are too closely accompanied by guns and battleships for them to be true witnesses of the Lamb. I have never heard that the Church has ever officially condemned punitive expeditions undertaken to avenge the missionaries.

Personally, I should never give even as much as a sixpence towards any missionary enterprise. I think that for any man a change of religion is as dangerous a thing as a change of language is for a writer. It may turn out a success, but it can also have disastrous consequences.

11

The Catholic religion contains explicitly truths which other religions contain implicitly. But, conversely, other religions contain explicitly truths which are only implicit in Christianity. The most well-informed Christian can still learn a great deal concerning divine matters from other religious traditions; although inward spiritual light can also cause him to apprehend everything through the medium of his own tradition. All the same, were these other traditions to disappear from the face of the earth, it would be an irreparable loss. The missionaries have already made far too many of them disappear as it is.

St John of the Cross compares faith to reflections of silver, truth being gold. The various authentic religious traditions are different reflections of the same truth, and perhaps equally precious. But we do not realize this, because each of us lives only one of these traditions and sees the others from the outside. But, as Catholics are for ever repeating – and rightly – to unbelievers, a religion can only be known from the inside.

It is as if two men, installed in two communicating rooms, each one seeing the sun through the window and his neighbour's wall lit up by the rays, each thought that he alone saw the sun and that all his neighbour had was its reflection.

The Church recognizes that vocational diversity is a precious thing. This conception needs to be extended to vocations that are outside the Church. For there are some.

12

As the Hindus say, God is at the same time personal and

impersonal. He is impersonal in the sense that his infinitely mysterious manner of being a Person is infinitely different from the human manner. It is only possible to grasp this mystery by employing at the same time, like two pincers, these two contrary notions, incompatible here on earth, compatible only in God. (The same applies to many other pairs of contraries, as the Pythagoreans had realized.)

One is able to think of God at the same time, not successively, as being three and one (a thing which few Catholics manage to be able to do) only by thinking of him at the same time as personal and impersonal. Otherwise one represents him to oneself sometimes as a single divine Person, at other times as three Gods. Many Christians confuse such an oscillation with true faith.

Saints of a very lofty spirituality, like St John of the Cross, have seized simultaneously and with an equal force both the personal and the impersonal aspects of God. Less developed souls concentrate their attention and their faith above all or exclusively upon one or other of these two aspects. Thus little St Theresa of Lisieux only represented to herself a personal God.

As in the West the word God, taken in its usual meaning, signifies a Person, men whose attention, faith and love are almost exclusively concentrated on the impersonal aspect of God can actually believe themselves and declare themselves to be atheists, even though supernatural love inhabits their souls. Such men are surely saved.

They can be recognized by their attitude with regard to the things of this world. All those who possess in its pure state the love of their neighbour and the acceptance of the order of the world, including affliction – all those, even should they live and die to all appearances atheists, are surely saved.

Those who possess perfectly these two virtues, even should they live and die atheists, are saints.

When one comes across such men, it is futile to want to convert them. They are wholly converted, though not visibly so; they have been begotten anew by water and the spirit, even if they have never been baptized; they have eaten of the bread of life, even if they have never communicated.

13

Charity and faith, though distinct, are inseparable. The two forms of charity still more so. Whoever is capable of a movement of pure compassion towards a person in affliction (a very rare thing anyway) possesses, maybe implicitly, yet always really, the love of God and faith.

Christ does not save all those who say to him: 'Lord, Lord.' But he saves all those who out of a pure heart give a piece of bread to a starving man, without thinking about him the least little bit. And these, when he thanks them, reply: 'Lord, when did we feed thee?'

Hence St Thomas's affirmation, that he who refuses his assent to a single article of faith does not possess the faith in any degree, is false, unless it can be established that heretics have never possessed charity towards their neighbour. But that would be difficult to do. As far as we are able to tell, the 'perfect ones' among the Cathari, for example, possessed it to a degree very rarely found even among the saints.

If one were to make out that the devil contrives the appearance of such virtues in heretics in order the better to seduce souls, it would be going against the words: 'Ye shall know the tree by its fruits'; it would be arguing exactly like those who regarded Christ as possessed of a devil, and perhaps coming very close to committing the unpardonable sin, blasphemy against the Holy Spirit.

So likewise an atheist or an 'infidel', capable of pure compassion, is as close to God as is a Christian, and consequently know him equally well, although their knowledge is expressed in other words, or remains unspoken. For 'God is Love.' And if he rewards those who seek after him, he also gives light to those who approach him, especially if they earnestly desire the light.

14

St John says: 'Whosoever believes Jesus to be the Christ is born of God.' Thus whoever believes that, even if he assents to nothing else of what is affirmed by the Church, possesses the true faith. Hence St Thomas is completely mistaken. Furthermore the Church, by adding to the Trinity, the Incarnation and the Redemption other articles of faith, has gone against the New Testament. To keep in line with St John, it should never have excommunicated any except the Docetae, those who deny the Incarnation. The definition of faith according to the catechism of the Council of Trent (firm belief in everything taught by the Church) is very far removed from that of St John, for whom faith was purely and simply belief in the Incarnation of the Son of God in the person of Jesus.

Everything has proceeded as though in the course of time no longer Jesus, but the Church, had come to be regarded as being God incarnate on this earth. The metaphor of the 'mystical Body' serves as a bridge between the two conceptions. But there is a slight difference, which is that Christ was perfect, whereas the Church is sullied by a host of crimes.

The Thomist conception of faith implies a 'totalitarianism' as stifling as that of Hitler, if not more so. For if the mind gives its complete adherence, not only to what the Church has recognized as being strictly necessary to faith, but furthermore to whatever it shall at any time recognize as being such, the intelligence has perforce to be gagged and reduced to carry out servile tasks.

The metaphor of the 'veil' or the 'reflection' applied by the mystics to faith enables them to escape from this suffocating atmosphere. They accept the Church's teaching, not as the truth, but as something behind which the truth is to be found.

This is very far from faith as defined by the catechism of the Council of Trent. Everything proceeds as though, under the same name of Christianity and within the same social organism, there were two separate religions – that of the mystics and the other one.

I believe the former to be the true one, and that the confusion between the two has brought at the same time great advantages and great disadvantages.

According to the words of St John, the Church has never had the right to excommunicate any one who truly believed Christ to be the Son of God come down to earth in the flesh. St Paul's definition is broader still: 'belief that God exists and rewards those who seek after him'. Neither has this conception anything in common with those of St Thomas and the Council of Trent. There exists even a contradiction. For how could any one presume to contend that amongst heretics there has never been a single one who sought after God?

15

The Samaritans were in relation to the ancient Law what heretics are in relation to the Church. The 'perfect ones' among the Cathari (to take one example) were in relation to a host of theologians what the Good Samaritan of the parable is in relation to the priest and the Levite. In that case, what are we to think of those who allowed them to be massacred and gave their blessing to Simon de Montfort?

The Church ought to have learned from this parable never to excommunicate any one who practises the love of his neighbour.

16

There is not, as far as I can see, any real difference – save in the forms of expression – between the Manichean and Christian conceptions concerning the relationship between good and evil.

17

The Manichean tradition is one of those in which you may be quite certain of finding some truth if you study it with sufficient piety and attention.

18

Since Noah is a 'representation of Christ' (see Origen), a just man and a perfect, whose sacrifice was pleasing to God and saved humanity, and through the medium of whom God entered into a covenant with all men, his drunkenness and nakedness have probably to be understood in the mystical sense. In that case, the Hebrews must have distorted history, as Semites and murderers of the Canaanites. Ham must have shared in Noah's revelation; Shem and Japheth must have refused to share in it.

A Gnostic quoted by Clement of Alexandria (*Strom.*, VI, 6) affirms that the allegorical theology of Pherecydes (Pythagoras's master) is borrowed from the 'prophecies of Ham' – Pherecydes was a Syrian. He wrote: 'Zeus, as he was in the act of creating, transformed himself into Love. . . .' Could it be that this 'Ham' was the son of Noah?

What makes one inclined to think so is the geneaological table. The descendants of Ham were the Egyptians, the Philistines (that is to say, the Aegeo-Cretans or Pelasgi in all probability), the Phoenicians, the Sumerians, the Canaanites – in other words, the whole of Mediterranean civilization immediately prior to historical times.

Herodotus, confirmed by numerous indications, declares that the Hellenes borrowed all their metaphysical and religious knowledge from Egypt by way of the Phoenicians and the Pelasgi.

We know that the Babylonians derived their traditions from the Sumerians – to whom must consequently be traced back the 'Chaldean wisdom'.

(Similarly, Druidism in Gaul was very probably of Iberian and not Celtic origin; for according to Diogenes Laërtius certain of the Greeks saw in it one of the origins of Greek philosophy, which otherwise would be incompatible with the late arrival of the Celts in Gaul.)

Ezekiel, in a magnificent passage in which he compares Egypt to the tree of life and Tyre to the cherubim guarding it, confirms absolutely what Herodotus tells us.

It seems, therefore that the peoples descended from Ham, and in the first place the Egyptians, knew the true religion, the religion of love, in which God is a sacrificial victim as well as being an all-powerful ruler. Among the peoples descended from Shem and Japheth, some – like the Babylonians, the Celts, the Hellenes – received this revelation from the peoples descended from Ham after having conquered and invaded them. Others – the Romans, the Hebrews – rejected it out of pride and desire for national power. (Among the Hebrews, exceptions must be made in the case of Daniel,

Isaiah, the author of the Book of Job and a few others; among the Romans, in that of Marcus Aurelius, and to a certain extent in that of men like Plautus and Lucretius.)

Christ was born in a land belonging to these two rebellious peoples. But the inspiration which lies at the heart of the Christian religion is twin-sister to that of the Pelasgi, Egypt and Ham.

Nevertheless, Israel and Rome set their mark on Christianity; Israel by causing the Old Testament to be accepted by it as a sacred book, Rome by turning it into the official religion of the Roman Empire, which was something like what Hitler dreams[2] of doing.

This double – and well nigh original – defilement explains all the subsequent defilements that make the history of the Church such an atrocious one across the centuries.

Such a horrible thing as the crucifixion of Christ could only happen in a place in which evil very far outweighed good. But not only that, the Church, born and bred in such a place, must needs be impure from the beginning and remain so.

19

The Church is only perfectly pure under one aspect; when considered as guardian of the sacraments. What is perfect is not the Church; it is the body and blood of Christ upon the altars.

20

It does not seem that the Church can be infallible; for, in fact, it is continually evolving. In the Middle Ages, the saying 'Outside the Church there is no salvation' was taken in the literal sense by the doctrinal authorities of the Church. At any rate, the documentary records seem clearly to indicate this. Nowadays it is understood in the sense of the invisible Church.

A council has declared anathema whoever does not believe that in Christ's saying '. . . whoever is not born of water and the Spirit . . .' the word 'water' actually referred to the

2 Written in 1942.

material element of baptism. On this count, all priests nowadays are anathemas. For if a man who has neither received nor desired to receive baptism can be saved, as is generally admitted at the present time, he must have been reborn of water and the Spirit in a certain sense, necessarily a symbolical one; consequently the word 'water' is taken in a symbolical sense.

A council has declared anathema whoever professes to be certain of final perseverance without having had a particular revelation. St Theresa of Lisieux, shortly before her death, declared she was certain of her salvation, without adducing any revelation in support of this statement. That did not prevent her from being canonized.

If one asks several different priests whether such-and-such a thing is strictly an article of faith, one obtains different, and often dubitative, answers. That creates an impossible situation, when the edifice itself is so rigid that St Thomas was able to put forward the affirmation referred to earlier.

There is something in all this which does not seem to fit.

21

In particular, the belief that a man can be saved outside the visible Church requires that all the elements of faith should be pondered afresh, under pain of complete incoherence. For the entire edifice is built around the contrary affirmation, which scarcely anybody today would venture to support.

No one has yet wanted to recognize the need for such a revision. One gets out of the difficulty by having recourse to miserable expedients. The cracks are plastered over with *ersatz* cement, shocking mistakes in logic.

Unless the Church recognizes this need soon, it is to be feared that it will not be able to accomplish its mission.

There is no salvation without a 'new birth', without an inward illumination, without the presence of Christ and of the Holy Spirit in the soul. If, therefore, salvation is possible outside the Church, individual or collective revelations are also possible outside Christianity. In that case, true faith constitutes a very different form of adhesion from that

which consists in believing such-and-such an opinion. The
whole notion of faith then needs to be thought out anew.

22

In practice, mystics belonging to nearly all the religious
traditions coincide to the extent that they can hardly be
distinguished. They represent the truth of each of these
traditions.

The contemplation practised in India, Greece, China, etc.,
is just as supernatural as that of the Christian mystics. More
particularly, there exists a very close affinity between Plato
and, for example, St John of the Cross. Also between the Hindu
Upanishads and St John of the Cross. Taoism too is very close
to Christian mysticism.

The Orphic and Pythagorean mysteries were authentic
mystical traditions. Likewise the Eleusinian.

23

There is no reason whatever to suppose that after so atrocious
a crime as the murder of a perfect being humanity must needs
have become better; and, in fact, taken in the mass, it does
not appear to have done so.

The Redemption is situated on another plane – an eternal
plane.

Speaking generally, there is no reason to establish any
connection between the degree of perfection and chrono-
logical sequence.

Christianity was responsible for bringing this notion of
progress, previously unknown, into the world; and this
notion, become the bane of the modern world, has de-Chris-
tianized it. We must abandon the notion.

We must get rid of our superstition of chronology in order
to find Eternity.

24

The dogmas of the faith are not things to be affirmed. They
are things to be regarded from a certain distance, with

attention, respect and love. They are like the bronze serpent whose virtue is such that whoever looks upon it shall live. This attentive and loving gaze, by a shock on the rebound, causes a source of light to flash in the soul which illuminates all aspects of human life on this earth. Dogmas lose this virtue as soon as they are affirmed.

The propositions 'Jesus Christ is God' or 'The consecrated bread and wine are the body and blood of Christ', enunciated as facts, have strictly speaking no meaning whatever.

The value of these propositions is totally different from the truth contained in the correct enunciation of a fact (for example: Salazar is head of the Portuguese Government) or of a geometrical theorem.

This value does not strictly speaking belong to the order of truth, but to a higher order; for it is a value impossible for the intelligence to grasp, except indirectly, through the effects produced. And truth, in the strict sense, belongs to the domain of the intelligence.

25

Miracles are not proofs concerning the faith (proposition anathematized by I cannot remember which council).

If miracles constitute proofs, they prove too much. For all religions have – and have always had – their miracles, including the strangest sects. Reference is made to dead persons having returned to life in Lucian. Hindu traditions are full of such stories, and it is said that even today, in India, miracles are regarded as events of no particular importance because of their banality.

To affirm either that the Christian miracles are the only authentic ones and all the others are untrue, or that they alone are brought about by God and all the others by the devil – that is a miserable expedient. For it is an arbitrary affirmation, and therefore the miracles prove nothing; they themselves need proving, since they receive from the outside the stamp of authenticity.

The same may be said with regard to prophecies and martyrs.

When Christ invokes his '*kala ergal*', there is no reason for translating these by miracles. They can just as well be translated by 'good works', 'beautiful actions'.

He said: 'Without my works, they had been without sin'; but also, and putting the two things on the same level: 'Without my words, they had been without sin.' Now, his words were in no sense miraculous, only beautiful.

The very notion of the miracle is a Western and modern one; it is linked up with the scientific conception of the world, with which it is, nevertheless, incompatible. In what we regard as miracles, the Hindus see the natural effects of exceptional powers that are found in connection with few people, and more often than not in connection with saints. They thus constitute a presumption of saintliness.

The word 'signs' [or 'wonders'] in the Gospel does not mean anything more. It cannot mean anything more. For Christ said: 'Many will say to me: Have we not in thy name done many wonderful works? And I will say unto them: Depart from me, ye that work iniquity. . . .' And again: 'For there shall arise false Christs and false prophets, and shall show great signs and wonders: inasmuch that, if it were possible, they shall deceive the very elect.' In Revelation (13:3-4), the death and resurrection of Antichrist seems to be indicated.

In Deuteronomy it says: 'If a prophet comes speaking in the name of other gods, even if he perform miracles, he shall be put to death.'

If the Jews were wrong to put Christ to death, it was, therefore, not on account of his miracles, but on account of the holiness of his life and the beauty of his words.

As far as concerns the historical authenticity of the acts known as miracles, there are not sufficient motives for either affirming or denying it categorically.

If this authenticity is admitted, there are several possible ways of conceiving the nature of such acts.

There is one which is compatible with the scientific conception of the world. For that reason it is to be preferred. The scientific conception of the world, if properly understood, must not be divorced from true faith. God has created this universe as a network of second causes; it would seem to be impious to suppose there to be holes in this network, as though God were unable to attain his ends save by tampering with his own creative act.

If the existence of such holes is admitted, it becomes a scandal that God should not contrive some in order to save the innocent from affliction. It is only possible for resignation to arise in the soul at the affliction of the innocent through the contemplation and the acceptance of necessity, which is the inflexible concatenation of second causes. Otherwise, one is forced to have recourse to expedients which all end up by denying the very fact of the affliction of the innocent, and consequently by falsifying all understanding of the human condition and the core itself of the Christian conception.

Facts termed miraculous are compatible with the scientific conception of the world if one admits as a postulate that a sufficiently advanced form of science would be able to account for them.

This postulate does not do away with the link between such acts and the supernatural.

A fact can be linked with the supernatural in three ways.

Certain facts can be the results either of what takes place in the flesh, or of the action of the devil upon the soul, or of action on the part of God. Thus one man weeps with physical pain; another by the side of him weeps for thinking about God with a pure love. In both cases there are tears. These tears are the results produced by a psycho-physical mechanism. But in one of the two cases a wheel of this mechanism is a supernatural one; it is charity. In this sense, although tears are such an ordinary phenomenon, the tears of a saint in a state of genuine contemplation are supernatural.

In this sense, and in this sense alone, the miracles of a saint are supernatural. They are so on the same principle as that governing all material effects of charity. A gift of alms out of pure charity is as great a marvel as walking upon the waters.

A saint who walks upon the waters is in every respect analogous to a saint who weeps. In either case there is a psycho-physiological mechanism one of the wheels of which is charity – there lies the miracle, that charity can be a wheel in such a mechanism – and which produces a visible result.

In the one case the visible result is the walking upon the waters, and in the other case the tears. The former is more uncommon – that is the only difference.

Are there certain facts which flesh alone can never produce, but only mechanisms in which either the wheel of supernatural love or else that of demoniacal hatred enters into play? Is walking upon the waters one of these?

That is possible. We are too ignorant to be able either to affirm or deny with regard to this matter.

Are there certain facts which neither the flesh nor demoniacal hatred can produce, which can only be produced by mechanisms having among their wheels charity? Such facts would constitute unimpeachable criteria of sainthood.

Perhaps there are some. There again our ignorance is too great for us to be able either to affirm or deny. But for this very reason, if such facts do exist, they cannot be of any use to us. We cannot make use of them as criteria, since we cannot be in any way certain with regard to them. That which is uncertain is unable to render another thing certain.

The Middle Ages were obsessed by the search for some material criterion of sainthood. There lies the significance of the search for the philosopher's stone. The quest of the Grail seems to bear on the same subject.

The true philosopher's stone, the true Grail, is the Eucharist. Christ has shown us what we are to think of miracles by placing at the very heart of the Church an invisible and in some sort purely conventional miracle (only the convention has been ratified by God).

God wishes to remain hidden. 'Thy Father which is in secret.'

Hitler could die and return to life again fifty times, but I should still not look upon him as the Son of God. And if the Gospel omitted all mention of Christ's resurrection, faith would be easier for me. The Cross by itself suffices me.

For me, the proof, the really miraculous thing, is the perfect beauty of the accounts of the Passion, together with certain glowing words of Isaiah's: 'He was oppressed, and he was afflicted, yet he opened not his mouth . . .', and of St Paul's: 'Who, being in the form of God; but made himself of no reputation . . . and became obedient unto death, even the death of the cross. . . . He was made accursed.' That is what compels me to believe.

Indifference with regard to the miracles would not trouble me, were it not for the anathema pronounced by some council or other, since the Cross produces the same effect upon me as the resurrection does upon other people.

On the other hand, if the Church does not work out a satisfactory doctrine concerning so-called miraculous facts, a good many souls will be lost through its fault because of the apparent incompatibility between religion and science. And a good many others will be lost because, believing that God enters into the network of second causes in order to produce particular results with a particular intention, they impute to him the responsibility for all the atrocious happenings in which he does not intervene.

The current conception in regard to miracles either prevents the unconditional acceptance of God's will, or else compels one to turn a blind eye on the amount and nature of the evil existing in the world – an easy enough thing to do, evidently, from the depths of a cloister; or even in the world from within a restricted circle.

In fact, one notices a deplorable puerility in the case of a great many pious and even saintly souls. The Book of Job might never have been written, judging from the ignorance displayed about our human condition. For souls of this type, there are only sinners on the one hand, and on the other martyrs who die with a song on their lips. Which is why the Christian faith does not 'catch on', does not spread from soul to soul like a prairie fire.

Besides, if miracles possessed the nature, significance and value attributed to them, their rarity today (in spite of Lourdes and the rest) could induce the belief that the Church no longer had any part in God. For the resurrected Christ said : 'He that believeth and is baptized shall be saved; he that believeth not shall be damned. And these signs shall follow them that believe. In my name shall they cast out devils; they shall speak with new tongues; they shall take up serpents, and if they drink any deadly thing, it shall not hurt them; they shall lay hands on the sick and they shall recover.'

How many believers are there at the present time, according to this criterion?

(Happily, this text is perhaps not authentic. But it figures in the Vulgate.)

26

The mysteries of the faith are not a proper object for the intelligence considered as a faculty permitting affirmation or denial. They are not of the order of truth, but above it. The only part of the human soul which is capable of any real contact with them is the faculty of supernatural love. It alone, therefore, is capable of an adherence in regard to them.

The role of the remaining faculties of the soul, beginning with the intelligence, is only to recognize that the things with which supernatural love is in contact are realities; that these realities are superior to their particular objects; and to become silent as soon as supernatural love actually awakens in the soul.

The virtue of charity is the exercise of the faculty of supernatural love. The virtue of faith is the subordination of all the soul's faculties to the faculty of supernatural love. The virtue of hope is an orientation of the soul towards a transformation after which it will be wholly and exclusively love.

In order that they may subordinate themselves to the faculty of love, the other faculties must each find therein their own particular good; and particularly the intelligence, which is the most precious of all after love. It is, indeed, effectively so.

When the intelligence, having become silent in order to let love invade the whole soul, begins once more to exercise itself, it finds it contains more light than before, a greater aptitude for grasping objects, truths that are proper to it.

Better still, I believe that these silences constitute an education for it which cannot possibly have any other equivalent and enable it to grasp truths which otherwise would for ever remain hidden from it.

There are truths which are within its reach, within its grasp, but which it is only able to seize after having passed in silence through the midst of the unintelligible.

Is not this what St John of the Cross means when he calls faith a night?

The intelligence is only able to recognize by experience, in retrospect, the advantages of this subordination to love. It does not divine them in advance. It has not to start with any plausible reason for accepting this subordination. And, indeed, this subordination is a supernatural thing, brought about by God alone.

The initial silence, lasting barely a moment, which pervades the entire soul in the interests of supernatural love, is the seed sown by the Sower; it is the grain of mustard-seed, practically invisible, that will one day become the Tree of the Cross.

In the same way, when one gives one's whole attention to a wholly beautiful piece of music (and the same applies to architecture, painting, etc.), the intelligence finds therein nothing to affirm or deny. But all the soul's faculties, including the intelligence, become silent and are wrapped up in listening. The listening itself is applied to an incomprehensible object, but one which contains a part of reality and of good. And the intelligence, which cannot seize hold of any truth therein, finds therein nevertheless a food.

I believe that the mystery of the beautiful in nature and in the arts (but only in art of the very first order, perfect or nearly so) is a sensible reflection of the mystery of faith.

27

We owe the definitions with which the Church has thought it right to surround the mysteries of the faith, and more particularly its condemnations (. . . *anathema sit*) a permanent and unconditional attitude of respectful attention, but not an adherence.

We likewise owe a respectful attention to opinions that have been condemned, to the extent – be it ever so small – to which their content, or the life of those who propounded them, contains some show of good.

Intellectual adherence is never owed to anything whatsoever. For it is never in any degree a voluntary thing. Attention alone is voluntary. And it *alone* forms the subject of an obligation.

If one tries to bring about in oneself an intellectual adherence by the exercise of the will, what actually results is not an intellectual adherence, but suggestion. That is what Pascal's method amounts to. Nothing degrades faith more. And there necessarily appears, sooner or later, a compensatory phenomenon in the shape of doubts and 'temptations against faith'.

Nothing has contributed more towards weakening faith and encouraging unbelief than the mistaken conception of an obligation on the part of the intelligence. All obligations other than the one of attention which itself is imposed on the intelligence in the exercise of its function stifle the soul – the whole soul, and not the intelligence only.

28

The jurisdiction of the Church in matters of faith is good in so far as it imposes on the intelligence a certain discipline of the attention; also in so far as it prevents it from entering the domain of the Mysteries, which is foreign to it, and from straying about therein.

It is altogether bad in so far as it prevents the intelligence, in the investigation of truths which are the latter's proper concern, from making a completely free use of the light diffused in the soul by loving contemplation. Complete liberty within its own sphere is essential to the intelligence. The intelligence must either exercise itself with complete liberty, or else keep silent. Within the sphere of the intelligence, the Church has no right of jurisdiction whatsoever; consequently, and more particularly, all 'definitions' where it is a question of *proofs* are unlawful ones.

In so far as 'God exists' is an intellectual proposition – but *only* to that extent – it can be denied without committing any sin at all either against charity or against faith. (And, indeed, such a negation, formulated on a provisional basis, is a necessary stage in philosophical investigation.)

Christianity has, in fact, since the very beginning, or nearly so, suffered from an intellectual malaise. This malaise is due to the way in which the Church has conceived its power of jurisdiction and especially the use of the formula *anathema sit*. Wherever there is an intellectual malaise, we find the individual is oppressed by the social factor, which tends to become totalitarian. In the thirteenth century, especially, the Church set up a beginning of totalitarianism. For this reason it is not without a certain responsibility for the events of the present day. The totalitarian parties have been formed as a result of a mechanism analogous to the use of the formula *anathema sit*.

This formula and the use to which it has been put prevent the Church from being Catholic other than in name.

29

Before the advent of Christianity, an indeterminate number of men, both in Israel and outside it, may *possibly* have gone as far as the Christian saints in the love and in the knowledge of God.

Similarly, since Christ's time, in the case of that portion of humanity outside the Catholic Church ('infidels', 'heretics', 'unbelievers'). And in a more general way, it is doubtful whether since Christ's time there have been more love and knowledge of God in Christendom than in certain non-Christian countries, such as India.

30

It is very *probable* that the eternal destiny of two children that have died within a few days after birth, one of them having been baptized and the other not, is identical (even if the parents of the second child had no intention at all of having it baptized).

31

Among all the books of the Old Testament, only a small number (Isaiah, Job, the Song of Solomon, Daniel, Tobias, part of Ezekiel, part of the Psalms, part of the Books of Wisdom, the beginning of Genesis . . .) are able to be assimilated by a Christian soul, together with a few principles scattered here and there throughout the others. The rest is indigestible, because it is lacking in an essential truth which lies at the heart of Christianity and which the Greeks understood perfectly well – namely, the possibility of the innocent suffering affliction.

In the eyes of the Hebrews (at any rate before the exile, and save for exceptions) sin and affliction, virtue and prosperity go hand-in-hand, which turns Jehovah into an earthly not a heavenly Father, visible and not invisible. He is thus a false god. An act of pure charity is impossible with such a conception.

32

One might lay down as a postulate:

All conceptions of God which are incompatible with a movement of pure charity are false.

All other conceptions of him, in varying degree, are true.

The love and the knowledge of God cannot really be separated, for as it says in Ecclesiastes: *'Praebuit sapientiam diligentibus se.'*

33

The story of the creation and of original sin in Genesis is true. But other stories about the creation and original sin in other traditions are also true and also contain incomparably precious truths.

They are different reflections of a unique truth untranslatable into human words. One can divine this truth through one of these reflections. One can divine it still better through several of them.

(Folklore especially, when properly interpreted, is found to contain a wealth of spirituality.)

34

The Church does not seem to have perfectly carried out its mission as the conserver of doctrine – very far from it.

Not only because it has added what were perhaps abusive precisions, restrictions and interdictions; but also because it has almost certainly lost real treasures.

As evidence of this we have certain passages in the New Testament of marvellous beauty but which are nowadays absolutely incomprehensible, and which cannot always have been so.

To begin with, nearly the whole of the Apocalypse.

The passage in St John: '. . . he that came by water and blood, even Jesus Christ; not by water only, but by water and blood. . . . And there are three that bear witness in earth, the Spirit, and the water, and the blood: and these three agree in one.' The same St John's insistence upon the water and blood that came out of Christ's side.

The talk with Nicodemus is also very mysterious.

St Paul '. . . be ye rooted and grounded in love, that ye may be able to comprehend with all saints *what is the length, and breadth, and height, and depth*; and to know the love of Christ, which passeth knowledge . . .' Already Origen, separated from St Paul by so short an interval of time, comments on this beautiful passage in the most banal way.

The passage in St Paul concerning Melchisedec '. . . without father, without mother, without descent . . . but made like unto the Son of God, abideth a priest continually'.

The doctrine of the resurrection of the flesh. The living flesh which must perish, and the 'spiritual flesh' (*pneumatikê* – should we keep in mind the Pythagorean theory of the *pneuma* contained in the semen?) which is eternal. The relationship between this doctrine and the importance attached to chastity ('Every sin that a man doeth is without the body; but he that committeth fornication sinneth against his own body.' 'Meats for the belly, and the belly for meats: but God shall destroy both it and them. Now the body is not for fornication, but for the Lord, and the Lord for the body.') [What is here the meaning of the word 'body', so curiously placed in opposition to 'belly'?]

The study of Hindu doctrines casts a much more vivid light thereon than any Christian text that I know of. Christians have never said, so far as I am aware, *why* chastity (and more especially virginity) possesses a spiritual value. This is a serious lacuna, and one that keeps away a great many souls from Christ.

The relationship between the doctrine of the Redemption in which man is the end in view (and which, as Abelard very rightly observed, is quite unintelligible) and the apparently contrary doctrine suggested by the words 'God hath desired to give his Son many brethren.' (This would then mean that we had been created *because* of the Incarnation.)

The mysterious relationship between the Law and sin, expressed by St Paul in sometimes so strange a fashion. Here again, Hindu thought furnishes a little light.

The insistence shown in repeating such expressions as '. . . hanged on a tree', '. . . made accursed'. Here, there is something irreparably lost.

The extraordinary violence shown by Christ towards the Pharisees, representatives of the spirit of Israel in its purest form. Hypocrisy, narrow-mindedness and corruption, vices common to every type of clergy owing to the weakness of human nature, do not sufficiently explain such violence. And certain words which have a mysterious sound suggest that there was something else: 'Ye have taken away the key of knowledge.'

The Pythagoreans named 'key' the mediation between God and creation. They also named it harmony.

The words 'Be ye perfect, even as your Father which is in heaven is perfect', coming immediately after the words 'Your Father which is in heaven, who maketh his sun to rise on the evil and on the good, and sendeth rain on the just and on the unjust' imply a whole doctrine which, as far as I know, is not developed anywhere. For Christ cites as the supreme characteristic of God's justice precisely what is always brought forward (example of Job) with the object of accusing him of injustice, namely, that he favours the good and the wicked indifferently.

There must have been in Christ's teaching the notion of a certain virtue attaching to indifference, similar to that which may be found in Greek stoicism and Hindu thought.

These words of Christ remind one of the supreme cry uttered by Prometheus: 'Heaven by whom for all the common light revolves . . .'.

(Moreover, this light and this rain also possess probably a spiritual significance, that is to say, that all – both in Israel and outside it, both in the Church and outside it – have grace showered upon them *equally*, although the majority reject it.)

That is absolutely contrary to the current conception whereby God arbitrarily sends down more grace on one man, less on another man, like some capricious sovereign; and that on the pretext that he does not owe it to any man! He owes it to his own infinite goodness to give to every creature good in all its fulness. We ought rather to believe that he showers continually on each one the fulness of his grace, but that we consent to receive it to a greater or lesser extent. In purely spiritual matters, God grants all desires. Those that have less have asked for less.

The very fact that *Logos* has been translated by *verbum* shows that something has been lost, for *logos* means above all *relation*, and is a synonym for *arithmos*, number, with Plato and the Pythagoreans. Relation, that is to say proportion. Proportion, that is to say harmony. Harmony, that is to say mediation. I would translate as follows: In the beginning was Mediation.

(All this opening part of the Gospel according to St John is very obscure. The words 'He was the true Light, which lighteth every man that cometh into the world' contradicts absolutely the Catholic doctrine concerning baptism. For in that case, the Word secretly dwells in every man, whether he be baptized or not; it is not baptism which causes it to enter into the soul.)

A great many other passages could be cited.

On the one hand, the lack of understanding shown by a certain number of the disciples, even after the day of Pentecost (proved by the episode concerning Peter and Cornelius), on the other hand, the massacres brought about by persecution, explain this deficiency in the matter of transmission. Perhaps by the beginning of the second century AD all those who had understood had been killed, or nearly all.

The liturgy also contains words with a mysterious sound to them.

Quaerens me sedisti lassus must refer to something else

besides the account of the episode concerning the woman of Samaria in St John. By considering these words in relation to the theme of a great number of accounts in folklore, a vivid light is thrown upon the latter.

The idea of God going in quest of man is something unfathomably beautiful and profound. Decadence is shown as soon as it is replaced by the idea of man going in quest of God.

Beata (arbor) cujus brachiis – Pretium pependit saeculi – Statera facta corporis – Tulitque praedam Tartari.

This symbol of the balance is astonishingly profound. The balance played an important part in Egyptian thought. At the moment Christ died, the sun was in the constellation of the Ram and the moon in that of the Balance (Libra). Note that this sign used to be called the 'Pincers of Cancer'. Writers did not begin to give it the name 'Balance' until shortly before the Christian era (one month before, the sun had been in the Fish and the moon in Virgo; cf. the symbolical meaning attached to the Fish [*ichthus*].

If one ponders this Metaphor, Archimedes's words 'Give me a fulcrum and I will shake the world' may be regarded as a prophecy. The fulcrum is the Cross, point of intersection between time and eternity.

Sicut sidus radium – profert Virgo filium – pari forma. – Neque sidus radio – neque mater filio – fit corrupta. These verses have a very strange sound.

And the preceding strophe (*Sol occasum nesciens – stella semper rutilans – semper clara*) takes on an extraordinary meaning when considered in connection with a tale of the American Indians, according to which the Sun, in love with a chieftain's daughter who has disdained all suitors, descends to earth in the form of a sick youth, very nearly blind and miserably poor. A star accompanies him, disguised as a wretched old woman, the youth's grandmother. The chieftain puts his daughter's hand up for competition and lays down very severe tests. The miserable youth, though ill and lying on a pallet, contrary to every expectation, is alone successful in passing them all. The chieftain's daughter goes to his home as his bride, in spite of his repulsive appearance, out of fidelity to her father's word. The wretched young man is transformed into a wonderful prince and transforms his wife, changing her hair and apparel into gold.

One could not, however, attribute this tale to any Christian influence, it would seem . . .

In the liturgy for holy days, *ipse lignum tunc notavit, damna ligni ut solveret –* . . . *arbor una nobilis: nulla silva talem profert, fronde, flore, germine* have also a strange sound. These are magnificent words; they must have been related to a whole symbolism that is now lost. Moreover, the whole liturgy for Holy Week has as it were a startling flavour of antiquity about it.

The legend of the Grail suggests a nowadays unintelligible combination, doubtless brought about during the years which followed the death of Christ – although the poems date from the twelfth century – between Druidism and Christianity.

Note that the Church has never condemned the poems dealing with the Grail, in spite of the evident mixture between Christianity and a non-Christian tradition.

Almost immediately after the Passion, Herod was sent into enforced residence at Lyons, accompanied by a numerous suite in which there must have been some Christians. (Was Joseph of Arimathea perhaps among them?) The Druids were exterminated by Claudius a few years later.

The *Dionysiacs* of Nonnos, a poem by an Egyptian (probably a Christian) of the sixth century, but which only concerns itself with Greek gods and astrology, and yet bears some very singular points of resemblance to the Apocalypse, must have been inspired by some similar sort of combination.

(*N.B.* It concerns a king, Lycurgus, already referred to in Homer, who has treacherously attacked Dionysus unarmed and forced him to take refuge *at the bottom of the Red Sea.* He was king of the Arabs living to the south of Mt Carmel. Geographically, it can hardly be a question of anything other than Israel. If it were admitted that Israel was looked upon by the ancients as a people accursed because of having rejected the notion of the mediating, suffering and redemptive God revealed to Egypt, one would understand what is otherwise inexplicable: namely, that Herodotus, avid as he was of every curious detail of a religious nature, should never have mentioned Israel. Note that Israel was predestined to serve as

Christ's birth-place – but also to have him put to death. Note also that there are numerous accounts testifying to the fact that Dionysus and Osiris are the same God. If we possessed the Egyptian version of the story of Moses, we should perhaps receive some surprises . . .)

The *Rune of Odin* referred to higher up, if it is not earlier than all contact with Christianity, would doubtless represent the remains of a similar blending. It would not be any less extraordinary.

Were there, perhaps, at the beginning, some of Christ's apostles who understood the words 'Go ye and teach all nations' in the way which I believe to be the correct one?

35

The understanding of Christianity is rendered almost impossible for us by the deep mystery surrounding the story of those early times.

This mystery bears first of all upon Christianity's relations on the one hand with Israel, and on the other hand with the religious traditions of the *gentes*.

It is extremely unlikely that there were not in the early stages attempts at a syncretism analogous to the one dreamed of by Nicholas of Cusa. Now, there is no trace of any condemnation pronounced by the Church against such attempts. (Nor, for that matter, was Nicholas of Cusa himself ever condemned.) And yet everything has happened, in fact, just as if they had been condemned.

Beside the silly nonsense talked by Clement of Alexandria – who was no longer even aware of the close bonds uniting Greek classical philosophy to the religion of the Mysteries – there must have been men who saw in the Glad Tidings the crowning touch to that religion. What became of their works?

Porphyry declared that Origen had symbolically interpreted the Hebrew Scriptures by making use of the secret books of the Pythagoreans and the Stoics. Yet when Origen talks about Greek philosophy, it is with the evident pretension of refuting it. Why? Because it happens to be the rival shop across the way? Or is it for some other reason? Was he trying to conceal his debt towards it? And if so, why?

This passage from Porphyry clearly shows that the Mysteries were entirely made up of allegories.

Eusebius quotes this passage, and calls Porphyry a liar for having said that Origen began by 'hellenizing'. But he does not deny the rest.

Eusebius also quotes the most curious letter from Bishop Melito to Marcus Aurelius, written in a very friendly tone (*Hist.* IV, 26): 'Our philosophy was first developed among the barbarians, but came into full bloom among thy peoples (*Tols sois ethnesin*) during the great reign of Augustus.'

These 'barbarians' can only be the Hebrews. But what does the rest of the sentence signify?

Augustus died in AD 14. Christ was then a boy. Christianity did not exist.

'Our philosophy' – might that mean our *Logos*, the Christ? Did it have its flowering (that is, its youthful expansion) among the *gentes* in Greece or Italy?

The bishop adds: 'The best proof that our *Logos* developed contemporaneously with the fine beginnings of the Empire in the interests of good, is that it suffered no vexation under the rule of Augustus, but, on the contrary, attained to all splendour and glory in accordance with the wishes of all.'

We always talk about the 'hidden life in Nazareth'. Only we forget that, though it is indeed true that this life was a hidden one, strictly speaking we do not know whether it unfolded itself in Nazareth at all.

This is all we know through the Gospel about the life of Christ before he was baptized by John.

He was born in Bethlehem. When still quite a small child, his family took him down to Egypt. He remained there for an unknown period. (Joseph returned after the death of Herod, but there is nothing to show that this was immediately afterwards; some years may have elapsed.) When twelve years old he spent the Easter festival in Jerusalem. His parents were then settled in Nazareth. It is curious that St Luke does not mention the flight into Egypt.) At the age of thirty he was baptized by John. And that is strictly all.

This is again a very singular mystery.

A third mystery is that of the relations between Chris-

tianity and the Empire. Tiberius wanted to have Christ placed
in the Pantheon and refused first of all to persecute the Christians. Later on his attitude changed. Piso, Galba's adopted son,
probably belonged to a Christian family (cf. works of M.
Hermann). How are we to explain the fact that men like Trajan
and above all Marcus Aurelius should have so relentlessly
persecuted the Christians? Yet Dante places Trajan in paradise. . . . On the other hand Commodus and other villainous
emperors rather favoured them. And in what circumstances
did the Empire later on come to adopt Christianity as the
official religion? And on what conditions? What degradation
was the latter made to suffer by way of exchange? In what
circumstances was accomplished that collusion between the
Church of Christ and the Beast? For the Beast of the Apocalypse is almost certainly the Empire.

The Roman Empire was a totalitarian and grossly material-
istic regime, founded upon the exclusive worship of the State,
like Nazism. A thirst for spirituality was latent amongst the
wretched ones subjected to this regime. The Emperors realized from the very beginning how necessary it was to assuage
it with some false mysticism, for fear that a true mysticism
should arise and upset everything.

An attempt was made to transfer the Eleusinian Mysteries to
Rome. These mysteries had almost certainly – convincing
indications point to this – lost all genuine spiritual content. The
atrocious massacres which had so frequently taken place in
Greece and especially in Athens since the Roman conquest,
and even before, had very likely caused their transmission to
be interrupted; the Mysteries were perhaps re-manufactured
by initiates of the first degree. This would explain the scorn
with which Clement of Alexandria talks about them, although
he may at one time have been an initiate himself. However,
the attempted transfer failed.

To make up for this, the Druids and the followers of the
secret cult of Dionysus were exterminated, the Pythagoreans
and all the philosophers pitilessly persecuted, the Egyptian
cults prohibited, the Christians treated as we know.

The pullulation of oriental cults in Rome at that time
resembles exactly that of sects of a theosophical order at the
present day. As far as one is able to make out, then as now,

they were not the genuine article, but artificial creations designed for snobs.

The Antonines represent something like an oasis in the appalling history of the Roman Empire. How is it that they were able to persecute the Christians?

One may ask oneself whether under cover of the enforced underground existence genuinely criminal elements had not insinuated themselves among the Christians.

Above all it is necessary to bear in mind the apocalyptic spirit which inspired them. The expectation of the imminent coming of the Kingdom exalted them and gave them courage to perform the most extraordinary acts of heroism, just as the imminent expectation of the Revolution does nowadays in the case of the Communists. There must be many points of resemblance between these two psychologies.

But, in both cases, such expectancy also constitutes a very great social danger.

The historians of antiquity are full of stories about cities where, as a result of certain slaves having been granted their freedom by some tyrant for one reason or another, it became impossible for masters to make themselves obeyed by those that remained.

Slavery was such an unnatural state that it was only bearable for those whose souls were crushed by the total absence of hope. As soon as a ray of hope appeared, disobedience became rife.

What an effect must have been produced by the hope contained in the Glad Tidings! The Glad Tidings meant not only the Redemption; they meant even more the practically certain fact of the very imminent coming on earth of Christ in all his Glory.

In St Paul, for every recommendation to be kind and just addressed to the masters, there are perhaps ten recommendations addressed to the slaves, enjoining them to work and be obedient. This might, if necessary, be explained by the remains of social prejudices left in him in spite of Christianity. But it is far more likely that it was much easier to persuade Christian masters to show kindness than it was to persuade Christian slaves, intoxicated by the expectation of the Last Day, to show obedience.

Marcus Aurelius perhaps disapproved of slavery; for it is not true that Greek philosophy, with the exception of Aristotle, acted as the apologist of that institution. According to Aristotle himself, certain philosophers condemned it as being 'absolutely contrary to nature and reason'. Plato, in the *Statesman*, only conceives of it being legitimately employed in dealing with criminals, in the same way as we do in the matter of imprisonment and forced labour. But Marcus Aurelius had as his business that of keeping order above all other things. He would remind himself bitterly of the fact.

Catholics readily justify the massacres of heretics by citing the social dangers inherent in heresy. It never occurs to them that the persecutions of the Christians in the early centuries are open to the same justification, with at least as great a show of reason. Much greater no doubt, for no heresy contained an idea so profoundly disturbing as the practically certain right to expect the imminent coming of Christ the King.

It is certain that a wave of disobedience among the slaves of the Empire would have brought the whole edifice toppling down in the midst of frightful disorders.

By the time of Constantine, the state of apocalyptic expectation must have worn rather thin. Besides, the massacres of Christians, by hindering the transmission of the most profound doctrine, had perhaps – and even probably – emptied Christianity of a great part of its spiritual content.

Constantine was able to carry out successfully in the case of Christianity the operation Claudius had been unsuccessful in carrying out in the case of Eleusis.

But it was neither in the interests nor in keeping with the dignity of the Empire that its official religion should appear as the continuation and crowning point of the centuries-old traditions of countries conquered, crushed and degraded by Rome – Egypt, Greece and Gaul. In the case of Israel, that did not matter; in the first place the new law was very far removed from the old law; and then, above all, Jerusalem no longer existed. Besides, the spirit of the old law, so widely separated from all mysticism, was not so very different from the Roman spirit itself. Rome could come to terms with the God of Hosts.

Even the Jewish national spirit, by preventing a great many

Christians, from the start, from recognizing the affinity between Christianity and the authentic spirituality of the *gentes*,
was for Rome a favourable element in Christianity. This spirit,
strangely enough, had even communicated itself to converted
'pagans'.

Rome, like every colonizing country, had morally and
spiritually uprooted the conquered countries. Such is always
the effect of a colonial conquest. It was not a question of
giving them back their roots. It was necessary they should be
still a little bit further uprooted.

[Note, as confirmation of this, that the only pagan prophecy which has ever been mentioned by the Church is that
of the Sibyl, which the Roman tradition had annexed. (Furthermore, the fourth eclogue clearly shows that there really was a
messianic expectation in Rome, very similar to the one in
Judea and equally in the flesh.)]

Christianity, subjected to the combined influence of Israel
and Rome, succeeded brilliantly in this task. Even today, wherever it is carried by missionaries, it exercises the same uprooting effect.

All this is a mass of suppositions, of course.

But there is one thing which is a practical certainty,
namely, that people have wanted to hide something from us,
and they have succeeded in doing so. It is not by chance
that so many texts have been destroyed, that so much obscurity
surrounds so essential a party of history.

There has probably been a systematic destruction of documents.

Plato managed to escape it; by what lucky stroke of
fortune? But we do not possess the *Prometheus unbound* of
Aeschylus, which must have allowed a glimpse of the true
significance of the story of Prometheus, the love uniting
Prometheus to Zeus, already touched upon, but no more, in
the *Prometheus enchained*. And how many more treasures
lost!

The historians have come down to us with great gaps.
Nothing has been left of the Gnostics, and little enough of
the Christian writings of the early centuries. If there were
any in which Israel's privileged position was not recognized,
they have been suppressed.

Yet the Church has never declared that the Judeo-Christian tradition was alone in possessing revealed Scriptures, sacraments, and supernatural knowledge about God. It has never declared that there was no affinity at all between Christianity and the mystical traditions of countries other than Israel. Why? Might it not be because the Holy Spirit has in spite of everything saved it from telling a lie?

These problems are today of *capital, urgent and practical importance*. For since all the profane life of our countries is directly derived from 'pagan' civilizations, as long as the illusion subsists of a break between so-called paganism and Christianity, the latter will not be incarnate, will not impregnate the whole of profane life as it ought to do, will remain separated from it and consequently non-active.

How our life would be changed if we could see that Greek geometry and the Christian faith have sprung from the same source!

APPENDIX

André Weil, a scientist, discusses his sister with Malcolm Muggeridge

This conversation was recorded for and partly used in the BBC film 'The Life and Death of Simone Weil' which was produced by Vernon Sproxton and transmitted on Good Friday, 1973.

This was my sister's room from 1929 until the war, until the Germans reached Paris in 1940. Of course, during those ten years she mostly lived in other places, but it was understood that this was her room in her parents' apartment. They acquired this apartment when the house was built in 1929. Our early childhood was in Paris in various places, and some time before the war of 1914 we came into the apartment on Boulevard St Michel. Then during the war the family had a complicated history because my mother, a very energetic and wilful woman, insisted on following my father everywhere: he was a doctor mobilized into the French Army. She followed him almost everywhere even against strict military orders. And we went along too. Our studies were, one might say, greatly disturbed, essentially greatly accelerated, by that process. Instead of following the regular classes, we took lessons mostly by correspondence and did a bit at one school and a bit at another school. So we went quickly through the system without being retarded by the routine.

I suppose that would only work with two rather remarkable students?

That is very possible. We had considerable success in our classes, that is true.

There was a close intimacy between you?

Very much so. My sister as a child always followed me, and my grandmother, who liked to drop into German occasionally, used to say that she was a veritable *Kopiermachine*.

Your parents both spoke German and French equally?

My parents always spoke German between themselves when my sister and I were not supposed to understand, as a consequence of which we acquired a good deal of German and understood perfectly.

Your mother, one feels more and more, was a most extraordinary person: do you think your sister suffered from her perhaps dominating character?

It would not be wrong to call my mother in some ways a possessive character, rather than dominating, and except where she considered it an essential duty, my sister tried her best to entertain the illusion in her mother that she, my sister, was my mother's thing in a way, and certainly this caused a certain amount of strain on her which, joined with many other strains, eventually led to her death.

And perhaps could be regarded as a contributory cause of the migraine which she suffered from.

At one time she even apparently contemplated suicide to get out of it – that was some time before the war.

Anyway, there was this tense relationship between the mother and the daughter. I suppose it was partly that which made your sister feel that at all costs she mustn't let you know in New York when she was sick in London.

That was one main reason why she kept it a secret and made all her friends in London swear that they would not let her parents or me know anything about this.

So this tragic news came to you in New York without any preparation whatever – out of the blue.

It was completely unexpected. To the point that since I knew that the lady who had sent me the cable, Mme Closon, had had some mental problems at one time, I wondered whether this was a fantasy.

She seemed to have practically no interest in her appearance. One expects a girl to have some kind of consciousness of wanting to make herself seem attractive: it doesn't seem to have operated in her case.

Apparently it never did, as far as I could make out. That may have been the influence of her mother, because my mother, who had excellent taste in decoration, had on the whole rather poor taste in clothes, and she never taught my sister what most young girls learn from their mother: how to put on their clothes properly, how to use a little make-up and things like that. My sister certainly never learned that either from her mother or from anyone else.

I've seen it suggested that your sister had a great spirit of emulation in the matter of your joint studies, that she felt you were ahead of her.

Probably it was a passing phase, and it has been to some extent exaggerated by some of her biographers. She mentions that at one moment in her early life she was in complete despair because she thought I was so far ahead of her and therefore, as she expresses herself, that much closer to the truth. But I don't suppose that this was a constant mood with her.

Or that it had any very great effect on her attitude of mind.

It is hard to judge. Those things are easily exaggerated by biographers who have insufficient material at their disposal.

And who have read somewhat superficially some of the drivel that psychiatrists write in our time.

Undoubtedly.

But of course your subject was mathematics, and hers was not.

She acquired an interest in mathematics, a strong interest, but much later, as a consequence of her studies in philosophy.

Philosophy, of course, continued to be her chief preoccupation throughout her life.

Except that, as you know, in her later years this was very much coloured with religious thinking, and she certainly would not have drawn any line between philosophy and religion. She would have said that the two are practically identical.

Then there was this tremendous influence of one of her teachers, Alain.

Alain – Emile Chartier, who signed his books 'Alain' – was an extremely impressive teacher by all accounts: his students have kept very strong memories of him.

And yet he didn't write anything particularly important, did he?

He wrote a great deal, and it seems that his students were able to find in his writings a great deal of the personality that they had learned to love and admire.

It would be true to say, wouldn't it, that the two of you were not utterly solemn students, and that your childhood together was full of happiness and laughter?

Oh yes; and I think it's quite clear that my sister always had an excellent sense of humour: I hope I can say the same of myself. Traditionally, being in the Ecole Normale strongly develops the sense of humour, particularly a certain sense of humour which is known in France as *le canulard*, with all those who are not entirely allergic to humour. There are characters from the Ecole Normale who are very solemn. But certainly the traditional and specific sense of humour which is developed in the Ecole Normale was obvious and apparent in my sister. We used to play tricks and tease our parents, as many children do. We even invented some special tricks which are perhaps not quite so common. There is the story about the stockings which some biographers of my sister have presented as a bit of asceticism. The true story is that my mother already had some views about natural living and we took those views up with a vengeance.

She was what we would call a crank.

That's a little too strong. She would not have done anything that her husband as a doctor would have told her was not good for anyone's health. For a number of years we used to walk with bare feet and sandals, and then, as a special way of teasing her, when we were in a public place — say, in a street-car — we used to complain loudly that our parents were not buying stockings for us and that we were feeling bitterly cold. Everybody looked at my mother with great indignation and my mother just didn't know what to do.

I can remember reading that your sister was so distressed by the sufferings of the soldiers in the First World War that she would refuse to accept her chocolate ration, or give it away.

This again is not a true description of the situation. Of course, everybody was feeling the war very much, and it was suggested even by the newspapers that civilians would do well to do without sugar and chocolate as much as possible. My mother took this idea up, but without being at all strict about it, and she suggested it to us, and to some extent we took it up too – but probably not more than many French children at that time. Also there was during that war of 1914 this institution – perhaps peculiarly French, I don't know – the *filleuls de guerre*. Many soldiers were from the North and almost completely cut off from their families, so both my sister and I had each for a while a *filleul*: a soldier at the Front, to whom we could send small packages of this or that. We were encouraged in the idea of saving up on our sugar ration and our chocolate and so on in order to be able to send packages to our soldiers. My mother told the story to some of my sister's biographers, who made much more of it than it deserved.

Would you say it was really quite a happy childhood that you had?

Absolutely. My parents were both very happy together. My father was entirely absorbed by his profession as a family doctor, and as a military doctor during the war. He was a good old general practitioner of the type which is disappearing fast, and he left everything else in the family, in particular the supervision of our studies, to my mother. On this basis they lived very happily together as long as my father could practise medicine, which meant until the war. After that, circumstances made it impossible for him to practise medicine and he led an essentially unhappy life, even apart from the fact that very soon my sister died. My mother always saw to it that we got, wherever we were, the best teachers available. She even got us on several occasions transferred from one section of the lycée to another just in order to be under a better teacher, and she insisted that we did our school work – but without being more strict about it than any capable and intelligent mother would be.

This is something of a Jewish trait, one might say, this deep respect for learning and education?

You might call it that. Actually her father, who was by trade a merchant, was a very well-read man who knew Hebrew very well, and in the old days I have seen books of

Hebrew poetry written by him.

But there was no specific practice of Judaism in the family?

No, I even remember that during the war someone told me I was Jewish and I just didn't know what that meant. This is something that could not happen in the modern world, I'm pretty sure.

I fear not. People don't realize today how completely the Nazis polarized this thing. People don't realize how retrograde our time has been in this respect. Given that in the family there was no sort of religious observance, when did you first become aware of your sister's interest in this side of life?

This is always not as simple as it appears in the standard biographies. Before she became a student of Alain, she was exposed to a woman who was not directly her teacher but was a teacher in the same lycée, a Jewish woman converted to Catholicism. Apparently she made a strong effort to interest my sister in Catholicism, to the extent that my parents were worried whether she might not get converted.

They would have disliked it?

At that time they would have disliked it entirely. Being baptized was the most unpleasant thing that could happen to a person in a family with a Jewish background.

Even with their scepticism about everything else, this still lived in them – that it would be something terrible for a Jewish girl to be baptized?

They would certainly have expressed their opposition to it. But it never came to that. This woman was obviously a kind of fanatic, and I don't think that my sister was greatly influenced by this episode. Certainly as soon as she met Alain she had forgotten it completely. Then very soon she became actively interested in political questions. There is even extant an interesting document, which must have been written in her 18th year, in which she asks to be allowed to join the Communist Party. The letter stops in the middle of a sentence and was never completed – obviously for excellent reasons.

Alain himself was of course a standard anti-clerical, I imagine.

She got interested in leftist politics, but she understood

very early that things in Russia were going wrong. She must at that time have shared those ideas which you still find everywhere that Lenin was a wonderful person, a humane person, and that everything went wrong just because he was replaced by this horrible Stalin.

Which is another myth, of course.

She saw through it at a quite early stage. Certainly in the early Thirties she has several articles where she indicates quite clearly that she had thoroughly seen through this myth, and that, while Lenin's personality was quite different from Stalin's, at bottom the principles were entirely the same.

What about her views on Trotsky?

In the late Twenties and during most of the Thirties, she went on seeking contacts with dissident leftists and dissident Communist movements, and necessarily came in touch with some Trotskyites. I don't think that she was ever much impressed with their views and their tendencies, but certainly when Trotsky came to Paris and his friends in Paris just didn't know where they could find a sleeping place for him, my sister arranged for him to spend, I think, a couple of nights in this same apartment where we are talking now. They had a long conversation. Anyone who had doubts about my sisters's sense of humour would have had no such doubts if he had heard her tell about that conversation with Trotsky. The way that she told about political discussions, political meetings was always *very* funny. Her interview with Trotsky ended up with Trotsky saying to her: 'I see you disagree with me in almost everything. Why do you put me up in your house? Do you belong to the Salvation Army?'

Would it be true to say that in time she did become totally disillusioned with the idea of salvation for man through politics?

At a later stage. That would coincide more or less with the time when she became more actively or more accurately interested in religious subjects, which was the end of the Thirties, more or less, not very long before the outbreak of the war.

Were you aware of this going on in her?

I am not sure, but probably almost not at all. We had had conversations about such matters. One of the books that influenced her most was the Bhagavad Gita. This is her copy of a French translation, but she eventually learned to read it in Sanskrit and inserted in this volume a number of verses in the Sanskrit text in her own translation. She knew that almost 15 years before I had been learning Sanskrit, and we must have had conversations about that. I was not aware how close she had come to the Christian way of thinking until I saw her in America.

So it was really when she came over to America in 1940 that you first were aware of the Christian orientation of her thought. Did you argue with her about it?

I did not exactly argue because I was in some ways in sympathy with her view of things. I remember one particular conversation I had with her where she mentioned that there were a number of serious objections against her being baptized as a Roman Catholic, and I said: 'After all, your objections would be exactly the same if you were to convert yourself to Hinduism, Islam, Buddhism or almost anything else.' And she said: 'Yes, that's about my position.'

Yet subsequently one does get the impression that she committed herself somewhat more strongly to the Christian faith than that.

This is rather hard to judge. I think her view seems to have been that all religions were essentially one and the same. She would not at all have been a believer in what is known as syncretism, a mixture of religions. She thought if you are in one religion you would stay there and the choice of one's particular religion was, she might have said, more a social than a deeply intellectual matter.

Did you see much of her when she was in America waiting to come to London?

Quite a good deal, and we had arguments about whether children should be baptized. She argued very strongly in favour of it. One of the arguments she used was this: that if she had been baptized a Catholic, as a baby, she would not have had this problem with her intellectual views – that she could not join the Church and could not participate in the sacraments. She offered this as one argument in favour of baptizing children – before they are aware of what's going on.

I suppose she was also deeply preoccupied with the question of returning to Europe in order to get involved in the war.

She wanted to suffer no less than any one of those who were suffering for the cause in which she believed. Therefore she was making the most desperate efforts both in America and later in England to be sent over to France, preferably on the most dangerous missions.

Was she still advocating in America this rather crackpot idea she had of a kind of nursing service in the very front line?

It was still in her mind when she first came to America. In fact, she was looking for people to give her access to the highest authorities in America: she mentioned Roosevelt, which was not quite realistic.

Who was going to get her to Roosevelt?

She went to Maritain.

I rather regret having said 'crackpot' because it was a noble idea, but, you would agree, totally impractical.

The idea might have been a good one in the First World War, but the circumstances had become completely different. It was based on long conversations she had had with people who had been soldiers in the First World War and had been at the Front. It was not unrealistic in such terms. It had become so because it was a different kind of war.

Which she hadn't quite grasped.

Which she had not quite grasped, but I think she did grasp it, and her efforts were then directed at being parachuted into France to work with the Underground.

And for that purpose she had to get to London.

She had to get to London and André Philip brought her to London. At first she greatly admired André Philip, but then her last letter, where she explains her resignation from the Free French movement, is rather bitter about the whole movement.

That last letter is completely unknown and is most important, because hitherto it's always been assumed that her dedication to the Gaullist movement remained intact.

Well, obviously it didn't. I had already seen some signs of that before, but this last letter, which was written less than a month before her death, remained unknown even to me until quite recently. The letter was directed to a man called Louis Closon, whom you may have known, and it remained for many years in the possession of Maurice Schumann.

I confess it comes as no surprise to me: I was a liaison officer with the Gaullists in London and I have always thought that the terrific idealism of your sister would have fitted in very ill with the mood of most of those people. I don't want to denigrate them, but they were adventurers, they were engaged in a war, they didn't see the thing at all as she saw it.

You were right, except that already when she went to London she had no great illusions about the so-called Free French movement. I had none at all because I had seen the beginnings of the movement in London in the summer of 1940.

You landed there as a soldier?

Yes, and I stayed there for part of the summer before being shipped back to France, and I had no illusions. My sister had very few illusions. She had discussions with the Gaullists in America and what she disliked most of all was their total intolerance towards anyone who was what they described as a 'collaborator' in France: many of those so-called collaborators were perfectly honest and decent people who were doing their best under difficult circumstances. In fact, my sister mentions in a letter which has been published that the Gaullists were calling her a Pétainist, and conversely. She was of course condemned to be on bad terms with almost everybody – it was with her an old experience. Everybody considered her an enemy because she could see through them very quickly.

She was concerned with truth and whoever is concerned with truth, in all circumstances, is the enemy of everyone.

Absolutely. She was primarily a lover of truth. In a sense, one may say this was her highest value: but in a different sense it may not have been. I will illustrate this by another bit of conversation. She was once describing to me – it must have been in America – some historical theory, or a historical fancy of the kind that you find expressed in her late writings, and I said to her: 'This is a historical question. It must be discussed in terms of the evidence. What is your evidence for what you are saying?' She said: 'I don't need any evidence. It is beautiful, therefore it must be true.'

Going back to her time in London: presumably her greatest disappointment was that she was not sent on a mission to France.

She hoped very much that this would happen. She thought that by talking to people she would force her will upon them, even in order to perform what she must have known perfectly well would not be an efficient mission. I don't believe she thought she could do something important. She thought she would do something useful, but most of all she wanted to share in other people's suffering. I don't think she was what some people call a dolorist – she was not looking for suffering for its own sake – but when others were suffering, she wanted to have her share of it.

It's a strange thing to me, this particular point, because as I was mixed up with this business to some extent, I can see that what she asked for was totally impractical from every point of view, if only because of her Jewish appearance, which would have been disastrous. What astonishes me is that with her tremendously sensitive nature she should not have been aware that the reason she couldn't go was not because it might endanger her, but because it would inevitably have endangered the people she was to make contact with. This thought never seems to have occurred to her.

That is not correct. She was perfectly well aware of it, and in her letter to Maurice Schumann, she describes at great length how much thought she had given to the problem of not betraying any secrets if she was caught by the Germans and tortured as a secret agent. She had given considerable thought to it and in fairly realistic terms, if one may call this kind of thinking realistic.

But she hadn't seen the problem in its full magnitude, had she, because the trouble would have been inflicted on the people she saw? Anyway, heartbroken by this, she was put to this task of setting down her thoughts on the problems that would confront France after the war, which produced 'L'Enracinement'. Did she really believe that that was going to influence the Gaullists?

I don't think she gave any thought to that question. At the beginning, they were thinking of a new *Déclaration des Droits de l'Homme* and they suggested to her to work on this, which was a very limited task, in their view. She immediately took up something quite different, because she thought it was wrong to speak about human 'rights' : she thought there must be a *déclaration des devoirs de l'homme* and *des devoirs envers l'homme* – the duties of man towards other men. She started writing on this topic, and was so carried away by the subject that she wrote a whole book. I don't think she stopped for a moment to think whether this would influence people. I wrote her a rather silly letter saying she must take good care of herself, because the future needed her. And she answered back saying : the future needs me no more than I need it.

Would it be true to say that this strange phenomenon at the end of her life of stopping eating was connected with a kind of despair?

There was a kind of despair, but there too it's very hard to distinguish between fact and legend. She did not stop eating : she had gotten into habits where she was eating very little, certainly not enough for preservation of life, partly out of habit, because she was neglectful of her own needs as she had always been. It had always been necessary for my mother to be around her as much as possible to see to it that she fed herself, even in days when rations were not talked about. Then she had, in addition, made a kind of vow that she would eat no more than was allowed for by the official rations in France, which of course Frenchmen never did, for very good reasons. So with that idea and with that habit, she became incapable of eating more than she was used to. When she was taken to the hospital and they found some TB and naturally prescribed, among other things, overfeeding, she refused it, partly out of principle but partly, I suppose, because she was unable to put up with more food than she had become used to. That last letter to Louis Closon refutes completely the thesis of a kind of suicide on her part. It says : 'I am broken into pieces. The only people who could pick up the pieces and put them together temporarily would be my parents, and of course they are out of reach. But possibly

I and they will come together in Algiers.' That was her idea and her parents' idea : that they could all get together in Algiers.

So she was still looking forward to going on living?

Not very much. She was – to discuss things in Christian terms – entirely resigned to the will of God about herself. In fact, her whole attitude during her last illness may fairly be described as saying to God : 'If you want me to live, you will preserve me : if you don't want to preserve me, then I am perfectly happy and ready to die.' And so she died.

And you in America had no notion?

Absolutely none.